The children of Israel becan people around them and th happening again? Are Chris meadow of the trivia of a co. understand our post-modern ` exodus from it even while liv̶ ̶ ̶ ̶ ̶ ̶ John Benton calls for a radical discipleship and believes the particular way this will be seen in our day is in the grace of contentment which only the strength of Christ can give.

Peter Maiden

To *Marcus Watkins*
a good soldier of Jesus Christ,
who first suggested
that my work on consumerism
should be turned into a book

CHRISTIANS IN A CONSUMER CULTURE

JOHN BENTON

Christian Focus

Christian Focus Publications publishes biblically-accurate books for adults and children. The books in the adult range are published in three imprints.

Christian Heritage contains classic writings from the past.

Christian Focus contains popular works including biographies, commentaries, doctrine, and Christian living.

Mentor focuses on books written at a level suitable for Bible College and seminary students, pastors, and others; the imprint includes commentaries, doctrinal studies, examination of current issues, and church history.

For a free catalogue of all our titles, please write to
Christian Focus Publications,
Geanies House, Fearn,
Ross-shire, IV20 1TW, Great Britain

For details of our titles visit us on our web site
http://www.christianfocus.com

© John Benton
ISBN 1 85792 484 3

Published in 1999
by
Christian Focus Publications,
Geanies House, Fearn, Ross-shire,
IV20 1TW, Great Britain.

Contents

PREFACE

John Benton has written a timely book. Being a Pastor in Guildford, one of the richest towns in England, we might think that he is an expert on consumer culture. But he argues that it is universal and not confined to the leafy suburbs. We can see it in the huge new shopping complex in Gateshead and in the even bigger shopping centre planned in Manchester, neither of which have Guildford's image.

He is right too to argue that it is something quite new in the last thirty or forty years. I would date it from its first beginning, when the shop floor activists threw off the restraining hands of the trades union leaders and abused the tight labour market given by full employment to go for a wage bonanza which lost Labour the 1970 election. But it was thrown over completely in 1979, when the new Prime Minister abandoned the full employment policy and progressive taxation for a policy which made the rich richer and the poor poorer and put millions out of work.

British society didn't care and her party won four elections in a row. They won the fourth, because the Labour shadow chancellor, the honest John Smith, said that taxes would need to rise. Income tax had come down from 33 pence to 24 pence in the pound and he judged, as did the Liberal Democrats, that only one or two pence was needed to help restore the social services and full employment. Labour did not make that mistake in 1997. The political reality is that the haves are not prepared to sacrifice a penny of their income for the have-nots.

I've spent the last five years among the have-nots, the teenagers who in the last few years began sleeping rough, and the sprawling housing estates, which are now no-go areas for the police, their schools, public libraries and churches, surrounded by twelve foot steel spikes. Their only escape from their grey world is drugs and they get the money for that by thieving.

A consumer society is inherently unstable. Those who sacrifice community solidarity for money will, sooner or later, find themselves without either. Nationalist and Unionist lived together in Northern Ireland without much fuss for nearly half a century until the closure of a factory in Derry tipped a thousand people into the already high pool of unemployed and the balance between those with a stake in society and those without was tilted fatally in the wrong direction.

One of the most graphic passages in the Book of Revelation is on the end of a consumer society, as seen through the eyes of the merchants, who stand far off. 'When they see the smoke of her burning, they will exclaim, "Was there ever a city like this great city? In one hour she has been brought to ruin!" '

The angel who brought the destruction says, 'The music of the musicians will never be heard in you again. No workman of any trade will ever be found in you again.... Your merchants were the world's great men, by your magic spell all the nations were led astray.'

It fitted the city of Rome, which was destroyed by the Goths three centuries later, in 410. The church survived, but the rich and corrupt Roman civilization did not. Rome has not been the only ruined city and it will not be the last, because a godless consumer society always carries the seeds of its own destruction.

John Benton shows us how Christians must distance themselves. His words are timely. It is only too easy for churches in the leafy suburbs to ignore the plight of their poorer neighbours. If loving our neighbour means anything, rich churches should help the poor, both with money and with talent. We need networks of Christian action in every city in Britain. The secular humanists can scorn the faith of a comfortable church, it is harder to scorn the faith of a Mother Teresa.

Sir Fred Catherwood

INTRODUCTION

The world in which we live is two things at the same time. First of all, it was made by the living God and therefore it is full of good things which are a tremendous blessing to us. But, secondly, this world has fallen into enemy hands; Satan has come in and therefore the world is also a threat to us as Christians. Because it is a threat, when it changes, and our society has changed rapidly in the last thirty years, we need to keep an eye on what is going on lest we be taken unawares. The classic trio of the world, the flesh and the devil can change the way they express themselves.

Not long ago I found myself in Kenya doing some Christian ministry. While I was there I found out why lions are like submarines. After the conferences were over we enjoyed a wonderful two days in the Masai Mara game reserve and had an opportunity to watch lions stalking the wildebeest, impala, Thompson's Gazelle and other such animals. From a Landrover, we watched with bated breath the lions' fascinating approach to the herd. The herd was there in the sunshine thinking, 'Yes, we know where the lions are.' It seemed unconcerned and took little notice of the lions. But the lions sunk into the long grass and, with their wonderful ability to crawl on their bellies, hardly disturbing the grass, they were submerged so low that one could not see where they were. They moved with great stealth and suddenly they were running at the herd from a completely unexpected direction. The herd scattered – it had been taken unawares – but some died.

9

Our culture has changed. It has become a consumer society which comes at us from a different direction than twenty years ago. It creeps up on us in unexpected ways. We need to have our wits about us as Christians or, like the Kenyan herds, some of those among God's flock will be snatched. The Scriptures tell us that the devil is a lion going about seeking those he can devour (1 Peter 5:8).

Wealth in the West

Compared with the rest of the world, we in the West are rich. You may not feel very rich compared with Richard Branson or the Sultan of Brunei, but you are rich. In the last decade in Britain, the total land space given to retailing has increased by a fifth. Shopping is now the national pastime, it is what people do when they have leisure periods. Obviously, we all have to consume things to live, but now we seem to be moving towards a society which lives in order to consume.

People enjoy the whole involvement with choosing and buying. Somehow we feel secure and comforted through acquiring things. It is estimated that the average person receives a couple of thousand advertising messages per day from TV, radio, posters, magazines and the Internet through advertising and marketing. The world around us is changing fast. How do we, as Christians, handle this 'consumer culture' in which society is rapidly becoming immersed? What should Christian discipleship look like when lived out against the background of the consumer society? With God's help, this is the topic which this book will seek to address.

What is Consumerism?

Before we go any further, let me specify a little more clearly what is meant by consumerism. The modern world has been a materialistic society for a long time, probably during this whole century we have been moving in that direction. We could say, for example, that Communism was a form of *materialism*. It promised fair shares for all. It was centred around the economic theories of Karl Marx. It denied the existence of God and was interested only in material well-being of the community. That is one form of materialism. On the other hand, capitalism is another form of materialism. From a 'free market' perspective it pursues the goal of individual wealth and worldly goods. So materialism can take different forms.

But *consumerism* is a step beyond. It is best described as an exaggerated and privatized form of materialism. People have thought about things they can buy, the things they can have in their homes, for hundreds of years. But now those desires are massaged in a much greater way. Consumerism is something much more potent than mere materialism.

Firstly, like materialism, consumerism is centred on this present age, on this world, on our five senses of touch, taste, sight, hearing and smell. Consumerism is focused on goods and entertainment that feed our senses.

Secondly, like materialism, consumerism holds out to us material goods and services as a promise of happiness. People are tempted to put their hope in wealth and in material objects. Because he owned so much the rich fool in Jesus' parable saw himself as in control, safe and well set up for life. 'You will get happiness if you take hold of these,' is the message. The objects vary enormously, from houses and cars to holidays and pension plans. But happiness and security are said to be found in these things. In that sense consumerism is the secular hope.

Thirdly, beyond mere materialism, consumerism focuses on the power of personal choice for the customer. We like the feel of that power. It is not just that our material needs are being met or that there are many material things to possess, but in addition we are able to choose. Being able to choose what we want is a way of expressing ourselves and people get great pleasure out of it. This focus on choice and personal options, along with increased spending power, is the central change of the last few years. The world has moved. Perhaps it has done this almost without our noticing it.

Back in 1962, President Kennedy addressed the Congress of the United States on consumer rights. He spelled them out as the right to safety, the right to be informed, the right to choose, the right to be heard. Up until that point, production had been very paternalistic. The industrial producers' message was simply: 'This is what we have made if you want to buy it.' But then in 1965 Ralph Nada became a leading campaigner for consumer rights with his book against the car industry, *Unsafe At Any Speed*. He began monitoring standards in the USA and exposed companies where things were not being done properly. The age of the consumer 'watchdog' was beginning to dawn. In the UK we had the abolition of the retail price maintenance, the opening up of competition, and the gradual and then the very definite introduction of the market economy. We had the rise of *Which* magazine, introducing the whole idea of consumer rights. Investigative TV programmes which defend the consumer and seek to expose any unjust dealing by manufacturers are now enormously popular. All this may seem to have little to do with Christian discipleship, but hold on.

What has happened is that in the marketplace there has been a real transfer of power from the producer to the consumer. Instead of paternalistic producers manufacturing things as they see best, now they have to listen to the customer. And so the customer feels powerful. But that feeling of being powerful, of being able to choose how to spend one's money and be the centre of things, is massaged. The companies in the marketplace know that it is not just the material things that bring the enjoyment, but that the sense of power is very much part of the enjoyment people have when they buy something. So a very potent part of consumerism is pleasure through power. When we walk into a shop we take out our credit cards and the salespeople and shop assistants become our servants. We are masters, we feel like gods. And that feeling like a god is enormously seductive to us, as Satan knew in the Garden of Eden (Gen. 3:5). We can have anything we choose. With the credit card system we are tempted to spend money we have not yet even earned. Such is the pleasure of the consumer.

We can think of consumerism then, as another gospel – the secular good news. We can define it roughly as follows. Consumerism is that promise of happiness offered through material goods and services which capitalizes on the pleasure of personal customer choice.

Plus and minus

As Christians what are we to think of this? First of all, perhaps surprisingly, we should not be wholly negative. Why? Because, we must realize that Christianity is a materialistic religion. Unlike some of the heretics we find in the New Testament (1 Timothy 4, for example) who said, 'Don't marry, don't touch this food', because they believed that material things are evil, we believe that the material world was made by God and therefore there is a goodness about it. Yes, it has been hijacked by the Devil, but basically there is nothing wrong with the material world. Indeed, in the incarnation God himself took a material body. Furthermore, we believe that at the end of time, God will not do away with the material universe but will cleanse and renew it. Hence material reality is fundamentally good. So we need to be careful how we approach the whole area of possessions. We need not be completely negative about it. Surely we can see that. It is impressed upon us as we think of the many needy people in the world. One of the things we, as Christian people, would love to see is them blessed with material necessities such as food, shelter, clothes and sanitation. The material world is good when it is handled rightly.

But on the other hand, as we look at consumerism, we immediately see the need to be concerned in at least three areas – the areas of ecology, justice and spirituality.

First, Christians need to be concerned about *the world's ecology*. In the consumer society of planet earth, 20% of the world's population consumes 80% of the world's resources. But if the majority wants to live a throwaway, high-tech, high energy, high pollution lifestyle, there is no green technology that can possibly cope with that behaviour. It is unsustainable, for it is not the way God intended the world to be run.

Secondly, Christians need to be concerned about *justice*. I sometimes enjoy going to the new cinema in my home town. There are nine screens and I can choose between various films. As I go in I see the ice-cream stand with a multitude of flavours and combinations of flavours. There is nothing wrong with a night out sometimes, we do need to relax occasionally. But then not long ago I heard of a drought near Lake Victoria in Kenya and of the little boy who dug up a dead dog in order to have something to eat. He died from eating it. As I was at the cinema with its varieties of ice-cream, I thought: 'Hold on, is this just? Is it fair?' Conscience asserts itself. As Christians, we have to think about this. We don't need to be kill-joys, but we have to be honest about justice in a fallen world of need and poverty.

The third area of concern for Christians is *spirituality*. Because consumerism shapes our outlook, our spirituality is affected. The way consumerism shapes people's characters is not necessarily in tune with the way Christ in the gospel wants our characters to be shaped. For example, in a credit card society which tells us to have whatever we want *now*, how does a person learn the Christian grace of patience? Or again, how can consumerism's emphasis on material reality help us as Christians if faith is about being 'certain of what we do not see' (Heb. 11:1).

But also let me ask this question: 'What trips up most Christians nowadays? What keeps our Christian lives at a low level?' It seems to me that it is not often the big sins such as theft or adultery that erode the spirituality of the general mass of Christians. What really undermines us spiritually is that we are trapped in the by-path meadow of the trivia of a consumer society. The banal TV, with the distraction of sport and soap operas; our cluttered lives caused by thousands of choices that we can make, with every one of them distracting us and taking us this way and the other, so that we are not focused any more on the one great matter in life – our God. Consumerism robs us of our focus and it is that which chains many of us down in our spirituality. Although such aspects of consumerism are not necessarily wrong in themselves, they rob us of our focus.

These are the kind of issues that we have to face. The world has changed; it is coming at us from a new direction, and we need to be alive to this, otherwise we are going to drown under the avalanche of choice and materialism. Where can we start? We will start by thinking about consumerism and the God of creation.

CHAPTER 1

GETTING OUR BEARINGS

As we saw in the Introduction, we live in the new world of consumerism. How are we to approach this shopping centre culture as Christians?

We can begin to get our bearings by remembering God as our Creator and our Saviour. A crucial passage is 1 Timothy 6:17-19, where the apostle Paul gives instructions to wealthy Christians concerning the temptations and traps they might face.

[17]Command those who are rich in this present world not to be arrogant nor to put their hope in wealth which is so uncertain, but to put their hope in God, who richly provides us with everything for our enjoyment. [18]Command them to do good, to be rich in good deeds, and to be generous and willing to share. [19]In this way they will lay up treasure for themselves as a firm foundation for the coming age, so that they may take hold of the life that is truly life.

Two unexpected assumptions

How do we come at consumerism? Consumerism presents itself as a method of obtaining happiness – and people want to be happy. Therefore, the first truth we need to grasp concerns *the happiness of God*. Perhaps this seems a surprising place to begin. In verse 17 Paul encourages the wealthy to put their hope not in riches, but in God. At the beginning of this letter Paul has already used a remarkable description of God. In 1 Timothy 1:10-11 he talks about sound doctrine; doctrine that leads to healthy Christian lives that conform to the 'glorious gospel of the blessed God, which he entrusted to me'. Note the description, *the blessed God*. Some of the alternatives by which we can translate the word 'blessed' are 'fortunate', 'happy', and 'joyful'. 'Blessed' is the word which Jesus uses in the Beatitudes in the Sermon on the Mount: 'Blessed are the poor in spirit.... Blessed are those that mourn...' Such are blessed, happy, for although they may face troubles in this life, heaven is theirs! They are therefore to be envied!

God is the blessed God, the happy God. The gospel, says Paul, is the good news about the happy God. Do you always portray God as frowning? There is something badly skewed about your theology if that is your vision of God. A great part of God's glory is his happiness. The Father, the Son and the Holy Spirit are in fellowship with each other and are filled with a depth of joy in each other that is beyond our wildest imaginations. So although God may be saddened and angered by our sin, there is a joy in himself which is foundational and which nothing can touch. He is the happy God. That is good news for us.

Furthermore, this joyful, happy God wants to share his joy with us. In one of his very helpful books, John Piper, the pastor of Bethlehem Baptist Church in Minneapolis, points out that this is one way of expressing the 'good news of great joy' which is the Christian gospel.[1] Paul in verse

---

1. John Piper, *The Pleasures of God*, Christian Focus Publications, 1998.

17 speaks of putting our hope in God who richly provides us with everything for our enjoyment. God wants us to be joyful, he wants us to share his joy.

We see this first of all in the account of the creation of the world in Genesis 1. There we read repeatedly: 'And God saw that it was good.' But it almost seems as if God, when he has seen the goodness of the world he has created, says to himself: 'I'd like someone to enjoy this goodness', so he creates Adam and Eve and puts them into his world. Now it is '*very* good' (Gen. 1:31), because the man and the woman are able to share in the joy of God's creation.

We see the same emphasis of God sharing his joy with his creatures in the gospel as well. Why did Christ live and die and rise again and call us to follow him? One of the ways Jesus put it is this: 'I have told you this so that my joy may be in you and that your joy may be complete' (John 15:11). In the long run sin makes people sad because it cuts them off from God. Salvation brings forgiveness and eternal life, and therefore joy! Jesus speaks of 'my joy' being in his disciples. But who is Jesus? He is God become man. So 'my joy' is God's joy. Jesus desires that his joy may be in every Christian. Further Jesus describes his people as those who will enter heaven with the greeting, 'Enter into the joy of your Lord' (Matt. 25:21,23). That is the message of salvation.

We will not get things right unless we realise that God is the happy God who wishes to share his joy with us. Therefore, because of this unexpected assumption, we have to say that the desire for happiness that ordinary people have is a legitimate desire. Christians should not be seen to be against happiness. We do not help the cause of God and truth if we continually give the impression that Christians are kill-joys.

Very often Christians, seeing such worldly love of pleasure, make the mistake of concluding the pursuit of happiness itself is wrong. 'Look at what the world does!' they say; 'Perhaps we should suppress this whole thing about being happy in this life.' We can laugh sometimes about what we in our house call the 'cod-liver oil syndrome'. Youngsters who grew up in the early 1950s were given cod-liver oil once a day. It was designed to make one strong and healthy, but it tasted vile. With such a daily routine one got into the way of thinking that unless the medicine tastes unspeakable, it cannot be doing any good! We can easily think like that as Christians. But if we do, we are terribly wrong. That kind of attitude is wrong because God himself is the ever-blessed, joyful God who wants to share his joy with us. God wants people to be joyful.

Indeed, this desire for happiness in ordinary people is a point of contact for reasoning with them about God and the gospel. People do desire happiness and yet so often their experience is that none of the pleasures this world offers is really able to satisfy them. In his great book *Mere Christianity*, C. S. Lewis writes:

Creatures are not born with desires unless satisfaction for those desires exists. A baby feels hunger: well, there is such a thing as food. A duckling wants to swim: well, there is such a thing as water. Men feel sexual desire: well, there is such a thing as sex. If I find in myself a desire which no experience in this world can satisfy, the most probable explanation is that I was made for another world. If none of my earthly pleasures satisfy it, that does not prove that the universe is a fraud. Probably earthly pleasures were never meant to satisfy it, but only to arouse it, to suggest the real thing.[2]

We should not despise the world's search for happiness. That desire can actually be our ally in seeking to lead people to God.

So there are the two, perhaps unexpected, assumptions which we need to fix in our minds before we challenge the consumer outlook. God is a God of joy and the human desire for happiness is a legitimate desire. In approaching consumerism, we must grasp these truths, otherwise we become very heavy-handed.

Two foundational principles

But, having said that, 1 Timothy 6:17-19 lays down two foundational principles regarding how are we to pursue joy legitimately.

First of all, we are to put our hope in God rather than material things:

Command those who are rich in this present world not to be arrogant, nor to put their hope in wealth [and all the things that wealth gives], which is so uncertain, but to put their hope in God who richly provides us with everything for our enjoyment.

The word 'hope' describes the happy anticipation of good. When we hope for something, we are anticipating a coming blessing. For many people, their hope is set on

---

2. C. S. Lewis, *Mere Christianity*, Collins, 1990, p. 118.

material things. They look forward to Christmas or birthday presents or to their next summer holiday. These things fill their horizons. This attitude is not for the Christian. His hope must be centred on God. Yes, he may look forward to a holiday, but that is secondary. The great day he anticipates is the coming of the Lord. He anticipates Christ's joy. The relationship he treasures above all others is his relationship with God. He looks forward to meeting with him and knowing his love poured out in his heart by the Holy Spirit. His hope is in God. Even the material joys and blessings he experiences in this life he sees as coming from God's hand. He looks to God, not the things he can buy, as the source of happiness.

Now Paul underlines that we are fools if we plant our hope in this world and what it offers. We will be fools because the pleasures of wealth are so uncertain (v. 17), they are passing. We cannot take money with us beyond the grave. Again we can think of the rich fool in Jesus' parable. Just as he thought he was set up for life, death came. God wants us to have a happiness which is more lasting than the happiness that money and things can give us. He wants us to have an *eternal* happiness, a happiness that is forever, not just something that you have for five minutes and then you are asking, 'What next?' God wants us to have himself. He is the ever-blessed God, joyful, loving, radiant with life abundant, and he wants us to know him. We are made in his image so that we fit together with him. Our hearts are made for his residence. Don't be so foolish as to set your hope on the things of this world.

Also, Paul says, 'Don't set your hope on the things of this world because they make you arrogant.' Sadly, that is how it is in our fallen state. Money makes us feel secure and when we feel secure, we feel we don't need God and don't need to listen to him. It makes us arrogant enough to say, 'I know that is what God says, but I am going to do something different.' We behave in this way because we feel secure. Don't be surprised when those in the church who get very rich start drifting from the church. What is going on? It is the Lord's parable of the sower being acted out once again: 'Others, like seed sown among thorns, hear the word; but the worries of this life, the deceitfulness of wealth and the desires for other things come in and choke the word, making it unfruitful' (Mark 4:18-19). Sadly, it is arrogance; they are feeling so assured, that now it does not matter what God says.

The Old Testament warned of this same problem. So often wealth brings secularism. It brings people to a position where they think they have no need of God and can forget him as an irrelevance. Moses warned the people of Israel as they were about to cross over into the richness of the promised land of this very snare: 'You may say to yourself, "My power and the strength of my hands have produced this wealth for me." But remember the LORD your God, for it is he who gives you the ability to produce wealth.... If you ever forget the LORD your God.... you will surely be destroyed' (Deut. 8:17-19). The secularism of the last two centuries is not some phenomenon which takes Christian faith by surprise. It is what the Bible leads us to expect would happen with the rise of a wealthy society.

So don't be taken in by the seductiveness of wealth. Don't let your faith be thrown into doubt by the grip which secularism has on people. As Christians, we are to be different. To set our hope on wealth as the anticipation of good is a misuse of God's creation.

What is creation for? Creation is there, says the Bible, to show us the glory of God. 'The heavens declare the glory of God' (Psalm 19:1). Romans 1:20 says the same thing: 'since the creation of the world, God's divine nature, his eternal power have been shown to us through what has been made.' Creation is there for our joy, but it is not there as a tribute to itself. It is there to cause us to realize: 'Wow, if this is what God made, what must God be like?' Creation is there as a stepping stone to true joy.

Romans 1 also tells us that in our fallen state we tend to worship the creature, material things, rather than the Creator, and that to do so is a misuse of creation. Yes, we should enjoy creation, but only as a signpost to direct us to the full joy in God. This is why Paul says: 'Command those who are rich in this present world not to be arrogant, nor to put their hope in wealth, which is so uncertain, but to put their hope in God, who richly provides us with everything for our enjoyment.' Through the gospel, God has opened himself up, that we may know him and enjoy his fellowship. 'I sought the LORD and he answered me, he delivered me from all my fears. Taste and see that the LORD is good; blessed, happy is the man who takes refuge in him. In your presence is the fullness of joy and at your right hand are pleasures for ever more,' says the Psalmist (34:4, 8; 16:11).

God opens himself up to our enjoyment, and this is seen very clearly in the teachings of Jesus: 'Come to me, all you who are weary and burdened, and I will give you rest. Take my yoke upon you and learn from me, for I am gentle and humble in heart, and you will find rest for your souls'

(Matt. 11:28-29). Rest is a picture of contentment and restoration of our life and joy.

Again, Jesus says: 'I am the bread of life. He who comes to me will never go hungry, and he who believes in me will never be thirsty' (John 6:35). It is a picture of sumptuousness. It is a picture of an energy-giving meal. Each Christian experiences times when he draws near to God and has his soul filled by the God whose loving kindness is better than life.

The Puritan Thomas Watson says: 'There is as much difference between spiritual joys and earthly joys as between a banquet which is eaten and one that is merely painted on the wall as a picture.' The one on the wall might look very good, but you can't eat it. Perhaps we should update that idea. You can see the mouthwatering photographs of the dishes in Delia Smith's cookery book, but those photographs can never satisfy your hunger. Just so, the things of this material world look so alluring, but can never satisfy our souls. Only Jesus can do that.

But also, when we pursue God as our focus in life, and find our joy in him, then the things of creation fall into place. We can use this world as a stepping stone to God and so enjoy the creation itself, but we are not trapped by it, we are masters of it under God:

> Heaven above is softer blue,
> > earth around it sweeter green,
> Something lives in every hue,
> > Christless eyes have never seen,
> Birds with gladder songs o'erflow,
> > flowers with deeper beauty shine,
> Since I know what now I know,
> > that I am his and he is mine.

25

So, to put our hope first of all in God rather than material things is the first principle Paul mentions.

The second foundational principle is to use the material of this world in the light of the world to come: 'Command them to do good, to be rich in good deeds, and to be generous and willing to share. *In this way they will lay up treasure for themselves as a firm foundation for the coming age*' (verse 18). We are to use this present world in the light of eternity. When God gives us material possessions, he is giving us the opportunity to lay up for ourselves blessings in heaven.

The heavenly treasure consists of various things. One will be the welcome of the Lord if we have been his good and faithful servants, willing to sacrifice the things of this life in pursuing his glory. Another will be the enthusiastic reception into heaven from those who have benefited from our gifts. Maybe you have given to a missionary cause, people have been converted through the missionary, and they have died before you. You enter heaven and hear them say: 'Without your giving, I would not have been saved. You enabled a missionary to come, I heard the gospel and I am here through your gift (as a secondary cause). Thank you!'

That giving which leads to treasure in heaven is a living proof to us *now* that we really do have eternal life. It shows us and others that we have really taken hold of it. How? From the fact that we are prepared to let the things of this world go. That is the proof that we have really taken hold on heaven and we have set our hopes on the world to come. God's people have this mark. We are not saved by our good works, but having been saved, we take heaven seriously and therefore live in the light of it and use the things of this world in a different way. The evidence of our regeneration is that we are using the things of this world in the light of eternity.

This outlook has evangelistic power as well. The New Testament challenges us to live lives that provoke other people to ask: 'What's different about you? What is this faith you have?' Here is one of the answers. We are to live differently from the world with respect to our wealth. Then they will ask, 'Why are you are using money in that way when you could have bought an expensive car? How come you are giving your money away, when you could be holidaying in the Bahamas?' Money talks to the non-Christian. May we use it to make them ask: 'What is the difference between you and me?'

Here then is where we need to start with regard to this matter of consumerism and the kind of society in which we live. There are two assumptions: God is the happy God, and the human desire for happiness is a legitimate desire. There are two foundational principles: our desire for happiness should lead us to hope in God and we are to use this world's goods in the light of eternity.

What do you really love? From what do you draw your buzz, your joy? Henry Scougal says in his book, *The Life of God in the Soul of Man*: 'The worth and excellency of the soul is measured by the object of its love.'[3] To set our hopes on material things is to devalue ourselves, to demean ourselves. To set our hopes, our love, on the greatest object in the whole universe, on God himself – with all his majesty, with all his virtues, and with all his power and glory – is to

---

3. Henry Scougal, *The Life of God in the Soul of Man*, Christian Focus, 1996. p. 68

expand our lives immeasurably. If he is the object of our love, then that places us in a different category from other people. The worth and excellency of a soul is measured by the object of its love. What do you love? What do I love?

CHAPTER 2

POST-MODERNISM AND
THE CULT OF THE INDIVIDUAL

One of my favourite pastimes, whenever I get the opportunity, is to walk by the sea. With the changing seasons the scene is always different. Sometimes the ocean seems blue, calm and placid like a mill-pond. On blowy autumn days, beneath the frowning skies, the sea is grey and the waves come crashing in.

The sea is one of the metaphors which the Bible uses to describe the nations of the world. We meet this particularly in the Book of Revelation and in the Psalms. The reason Scripture uses this metaphor is because, just as the sea is always changing, always on the move, so too are the nations and cultures of the earth. There are tides and times in the affairs of men. Empires rise and fall. Societies evolve and decline. Civilizations ebb and flow, come and go.

No consideration of living as a Christian in the contemporary world could be complete without addressing the fact that we live in a time of tremendous cultural change. The countries of the world are altering under the continual advance of technology and the differing currents of political opinion. We have seen both the rise and the collapse of Communism in the twentieth century, and it remains to be seen which path many lands will take in the future.

In particular, in the Western world we are living through

a period of gigantic cultural upheaval. Commentators tell us that we have begun to enter the 'post-modern' era. This is more than a trendy piece of socio-speak. The world on the brink of the twenty-first century is fundamentally different from that which immediately followed World War II. Views, values and visions of life have changed dramatically and, along with the burgeoning drive of industrialization and increasing wealth, these new ideas have contributed markedly to the rise of the consumer society. To understand the consumer mentality we need to try to understand where we are and grapple with how we have come to be there.

What is post-modernism?

The 'post' of the post-modern world indicates that we are living in a society which is somehow 'after' the modern world. Of course, linguistically this is nonsense; whatever is current is by definition modern. But the word 'modern' is being used in a different sense here.

'Modern' refers to the outlook of 'modernism'. Modernism is the label given to a cluster of ideas associated with the so-called Enlightenment of the seventeenth and eighteenth centuries in Europe. It proclaimed that man had 'come of age' and no longer needed foolish infant ideas such as belief in God. We were our own masters. Above all, science and human reason would produce a good and just society. We needed nothing else but to observe and to think. This would bring human beings the liberty they need. The Enlightenment produced an optimistic faith in progress. Free from the deception and oppression of religion, people would be free thinking and prosper under the light of rationalism. This was the vision of the modern age.

But because that optimistic vision of modernism is beginning to crumble, we now live in a post-modern world. People are losing faith in the idea that human wisdom alone can solve all mankind's problems. We are moving away from believing in universal objective truth and certainty. The idea that morality, for example, should be the same for everyone in every age is looked on as ridiculous. Somehow we are moving into a way of thinking which is less certain and the irrational has much more place in people's lives. Science and rational thought are not seen as the saviours of mankind which they were once thought to be. Human beings have deeper needs. We have become part of an age where people believe that what we feel is more important than what we think.

The impulses behind this shift to a post-modern mindset are various and complex. I am not sure that we can ever fully list all the reasons as to why this change has occurred. However, let us try to sketch out a few of the major ones.

Why the change?
1. At the practical level many people see that science has perhaps created as many problems for the world as it has solved. Technological industry has brought global warming and drastically damaged the environment, and if this trend is not reversed it appears it may threaten the very continuance of life on earth. Faster travel and communication have made many people's lives more pressurized. The advent of computers and robotic factories have increased unemployment. Our modern cities, for all their amenities,

are often places of violence, injustice, anonymity and decay.

The idea of science has also been brought into disrepute in the popular mind also by the suspicion of 'experts'. Both defence and prosecution lawyers in many criminal cases seem to be able to summon forensic scientists who draw different conclusions from the same evidence. Science is not the great arbiter of truth it once appeared to be.

2. Some would argue that ideologies which have been certain that they have 'the truth' have produced a good deal of harm in the world as they have tried to impose 'the truth' on other people. The closed mind of 'scientific' Marxism led many to the Russian gulags and the Cambodian killing fields. Similarly, some point the finger at the major religions and the institutionalized church as the cause of religious wars and sectarian violence in many parts of the world. This too militates against the very idea of being certain of the truth. They would say that all this 'certainty' has led to trouble, and perhaps it has done so because the very idea of 'truth' that is true for everyone is itself a phantom. With these kinds of ideas in the air, is it surprising that a post-modern mindset has begun to take over?

3. At the individual level, people find that there is a spiritual vacuum inside them, which no amount of science and rationalism can satisfy. The modern world has not been a happy world. For all our increase in standards of living we find that, for example, in Britain between a quarter and a third of all visits to doctors are to do with depression or some other form of mental problems. People are looking for something more than the modern world offers. Hence

we have seen the rise of 'consumer religion', namely, the New Age movement. People must be left to find, not absolute truth, but what is 'true for me'. Here again we see the post-modern move from objective truth towards subjectivism.

4. With the rise of technology, particularly computers, we have become accustomed to using machines which work, yet at the same time are far too complex for most of us to understand. Perhaps this, in and of itself, has made ordinary people used to the idea of a fragmented, incoherent view of life. 'Some bits I can understand and some bits I can't. There is no point in looking for an over-arching, comprehensive view of life. All that matters is being able to make things work for me.' This is the post-modern outlook.

5. We live in a society which has produced information technology. There are not only magazines, newspapers, cinema and TV, there are also the internet, fax-machines, CD inputs, e-mail... and the list could go on. We are constantly bombarded by information on all kinds of subjects. This overload of information has led many people to give up on old fashioned, reasoned decision making.

For every product which is introduced to you, there is always another with other advantages. For every political argument put forward, there are always another five or six points of view which seem equally cogent. With this overload of information many people have given up on using their minds to make decisions. It is too complicated to sift through all the data. Post-modern people have subconsciously come to the conclusion that a far easier way to make decisions is to go on their feelings. 'Do I feel good or bad about this person or proposal?' It is much simpler to answer that question, and even if I did take time to stop and think, things are so complex that I may well get it wrong anyway. There is also something romantic about following your heart rather than your head, which appeals to people and reinforces this way of living. So again, we can see that along these lines, logic and the modernist idea of objective, rational truth is set aside.

6. At a more theoretical and philosophical level, post-modernism is taking over from the modern view of the world, because (without God) the secular, modern ideas of universal truth have been shown to be vulnerable on their own terms.

Linguistic philosophers insist that any propositional statement can be 'deconstructed'. That is, it can be unravelled to expose hidden motives behind why it was made by those who made it, and when minutely scrutinized it can be shown to be self-contradictory to some extent.

The source of this vulnerability is that modernity always saw truth in terms of absolute precision. But contemporary thinkers have gone out of their way to show that no word statement has an absolutely precise meaning. It is similar to the fact that mathematically we can never know the precise length of the circumference of something as simple as a circle. Although a circle is such an everyday object, yet because the value of 'pi' has an infinite number of decimal places, absolute precision is impossible. Contemporary thinkers have pushed the idea that if precision is impossible in word statements, then a certainty about 'truth' is also impossible.

With this theoretical foundation, people's innate suspicion of authority is given extra strength. Authority is perceived as something which threatens personal freedom. In this atmosphere the so-called 'hermeneutics of suspicion' have developed. All truth is seen as something that has been constructed by self-interested groups of people, in order for them to maintain their power and status over against other people. So, for example, the idea of monogamous heterosexual marriage as the right way for society is represented as just an idea foisted on us to oppress deviants and maintain the status quo for the church and those in power. Or again, modern science and medicine is seen as simply a Western construct for the domination of the rest of the world and the sidelining of alternative societies. The message is, 'You can't trust what others tell you is the truth.'

The conditioning which leads groups to construct their versions of 'universal truth' is made up of such an infinite variety of factors that we can never finally break through to any absolutes which might lie at the root of it all. We live therefore in an age which is sometimes called post-ideological. Our contemporaries are suspicious of any grand theories of life, from whatever stable they happen to come.

7. The present world has become a small world with the advent of jet travel and telecommunications. This has led to a constant and deep inter-flow of people from one country to another. We have thus been exposed to a great many new ideas and cultural values as the races, religions and

cultures of the world mix together. This too has led to questioning the old idea of universal truth. Seeing how others think about life and living has caused people to question their own ways and values. The thought inevitably occurs that perhaps no one has overall truth. Enlightenment views of truth are just part of a 'Western mindset'.

All these factors and more have been working against the old ideas of objective truth, and so have catapulted us into the post-modern world.

The way we see things

It needs to be said, of course, that this whole post-modern outlook is open to doubt on its own terms. If truth is a construct, then perhaps post-modernism is itself a construct, developed to serve the purposes of the current academic establishment and the multi-national media manipulators. It is also worth noting that when people raise questions concerning the so-called 'Western mindset' they usually are looking for answers in terms of objective statements and logic, namely, the Western mindset!

But be that as it may, the point is that currently the post-modern outlook is beginning to deeply touch and shape the views of ordinary people. Rationalism, having failed, is giving way to emotionalism, subjectivism and sometimes irrationality. Everything becomes relativised. It all depends on 'the way I see it'.

What matters, therefore, above everything else for the individual is what is 'true for me' and what 'works for me'. And the post-modern definition of what 'works for me' is 'that which gives me a sense of well-being and pleasure'. Because this way of approaching life is essentially subjective and feelings orientated, then post-modern culture can be described as a therapeutic culture. It is a society in which the psychological sense of feeling good about oneself and about life is the controlling priority. In a way it does not even matter if I am told lies (if there is no truth, what is a lie?), as long as those lies make me feel good. After all, the contemporary secularist would say there is only this life and you can only live it once, and the only purpose is to enjoy yourself while you can.

Thus the cultural air we breathe fosters what we might call the cult of individualism and is extremely fertile soil for the consumer mentality. Indeed, so vitally intertwined is the post-modern mindset and consumer experience that perhaps it is not possible to say which one comes first. Does post-modern thinking pave the way for consumerism? It certainly does. Yet on the other hand it could perhaps equally be argued that the post-modern mindset has been invented in order to justify our consumerism.

Consumer mentality

In concluding this chapter, then, let us just spell out a few ways in which post-modernism and consumerism seem made for each other.

1. We have defined consumerism as a kind of secular gospel which offers the promise of happiness through material goods and services of the individual's personal choice. Consumerism's primary aim is to do with making the individual happy. Other consideration such as duty to society or old fashioned morals are sidelined. It parades the ideal of personal satisfaction. The customer must always

go away feeling good about whatever they have purchased. This central concern fits precisely with the post-modern therapy culture. In fact the idea that if you are feeling depressed or bored you can make yourself feel better by going out and buying something new is very prevalent at the popular level. Kill the blues by having a good spend-up. It leads many people into debt – but we give it the label 'retail therapy'.

2. The distinction we have made between old fashioned materialism and the idea of consumerism has focused on the matter of the primacy of personal choice. Consumerism doesn't just offer people things, it offers them a vast range of things from which they can choose. Part of the buzz of consumerism is the pleasure of personal choice. By personal choice we express ourselves and our individuality. Young people especially use their choice of clothes and music to make a statement about themselves.

In post-modernism's climate which tells us that the only truth is what is 'true for you', it follows that personal preferences are of extreme importance. Here again, consumerism provides the perfect foil for the post-modern outlook.

3. The post-modern world sees no value in history or in long term goals – that would be to give some credence to the idea of universal truth. There are no over-arching principles which are of lasting value. That being the case, post-modernism is not simply a philosophy which exalts the subjective, it is a way of living which prizes the tangible and the immediate. It deals in the materialistic currency of what you can touch, taste, see, hear and smell – what you

can experience *now*. It pressures people to live for the instant, on the spur of the moment. Its message is: 'Do it now, you may not feel like this tomorrow.'

The consumer marketplace offers satisfaction again to precisely that need. It offers things and it offers them immediately. It offers fast food. It offers instant credit. It tells you that you do not have to wait. There is no virtue in waiting. You can have things now. And *now* is all that matters. Whereas the generation living as adults immediately after World War II had lived through the depression of the 1930s and had largely accepted a way of life which saw benefits in frugality and saving, the post-modern generation is very different. There is an expectation of individual, instantaneous gratification which consumerism seeks to fulfil and exploit.

There is much more which could be said here. The emergence of industrial civilization, wealth, tele-communications and microchip technology have doubtless facilitated the rise of consumer society but did not make that rise inevit-able. The Western world with all its wealth could have taken other paths. It is post-modernism working in the minds of naturally self-centred human beings which has made us eager for society to go along the road of consumerism.

CHAPTER 3

WHATEVER HAPPENED TO THE COUNTER-CULTURE?

Please read: Luke 6.17-36

> ¹⁷He went down with them and stood on a level place. A large crowd of his disciples was there and a great number of people from all over Judea, from Jerusalem, and from the coast of Tyre and Sidon, ¹⁸who had come to hear him and to be healed of their diseases. Those troubled by evil spirits were cured, ¹⁹and the people all tried to touch him, because power was coming from him and healing them all.
>
> ²⁰Looking at his disciples, he said:
> > 'Blessed are you who are poor,
> > > for yours is the kingdom of God.
> > ²¹Blessed are you who hunger now,
> > > for you will be satisfied.
> > Blessed are you who weep now,
> > > for you will laugh.
> > ²²Blessed are you when men hate you,
> > > when they exclude you and insult you
> > and reject your name as evil,
> > > because of the Son of Man.
>
> ²³'Rejoice in that day and leap for joy, because great is your reward in heaven. For that is how their fathers treated the prophets.

²⁴'But woe to you who are rich,
    for you have already received your comfort.
²⁵Woe to you who are well fed now,
    for you will go hungry.
Woe to you who laugh now,
    for you will mourn and weep.
²⁶Woe to you when all men speak well of you,
    for that is how their fathers treated
      the false prophets.

²⁷'But I tell you who hear me: Love your enemies, do good to those who hate you, ²⁸bless those who curse you, pray for those who ill-treat you. ²⁹If someone strikes you on one cheek, turn to him the other also. If someone takes your cloak, do not stop him from taking your tunic. ³⁰Give to everyone who asks you, and if anyone takes what belongs to you, do not demand it back. ³¹Do to others as you would have them do to you.

³²'If you love those who love you, what credit is that to you? Even "sinners" love those who love them. ³³And if you do good to those who are good to you, what credit is that to you? Even "sinners" do that. ³⁴And if you lend to those from whom you expect repayment, what credit is that to you? Even "sinners" lend to "sinners," expecting to be repaid in full. ³⁵But love your enemies, do good to them, and lend to them without expecting to get anything back. Then your reward will be great, and you will be sons of the Most High, because he is kind to the ungrateful and wicked. ³⁶Be merciful, just as your Father is merciful.'

Arthur O'Shaughnessy was a poet of whom probably most of us today have never heard. He lived from 1844 to 1881. He used to work at the British Museum in London, in the Victorian era when great discoveries in science and ancient history were being made. But he wrote one memorable verse, which goes as follows:

> We are the music makers, we are the dreamers of dreams,
> wandering by lone sea breakers and sitting by desolate streams,
> world losers and world forsakers on whom the pale moon gleams,
> yet we are the movers and shakers of the world forever it seems.

This poem conjures up visions of lonely outcasts from society, who have a dream which is initially rejected but which eventually changes the world. O'Shaughnessy is writing using the metaphor of music. There have been many composers who were innovators, misunderstood and ignored in their lifetimes, only for their genius later to be recognized.

Yet it is not only in music but in all kinds of areas historically that we can find that kind of thing happening. In the military realm, for example, we can think of someone like T.E. Lawrence of Arabia, a loner, an unconventional person, an irritation to the establishment, but one who changed the course of World War I in the Middle East with his new ideas. People like him are outcasts, who are yet at the same time revolutionaries.

Now it seems to me that we find this description of Christians as outcasts who are revolutionaries in Luke 6. It is an image, a model, that we desperately need to recapture. Jesus speaks about his people being 'blessed', but being, at the same time, those who are insulted. They are outsiders to the world. Jesus speaks about a new way

43

of living, loving not just our friends but loving our enemies. That was and will always continue to be a revolutionary idea. The model of the revolutionary outcast is a blueprint for true discipleship. It is a blueprint we need to rediscover.

It was back in 1978, just before Mrs Thatcher came to power in Britain, that John Stott wrote his famous commentary on the Sermon on the Mount entitled *Christian Counter-culture*. But now, looking at the church twenty or more years later, I wonder, what happened to the counter-culture? How are Christians different? We seem frequently to be as much enmeshed and immersed in the promise of happiness that is held out by consumerism as anyone else. Some of the challenges we will face in this book, no doubt, we find very uncomfortable. But God's Word brings uncomfortable things to us. There is nothing wrong with the material world, but Christians are being drawn ever more deeply into the worship of created things. We can be finding our joy in created things rather than the Creator. Many who call themselves Christians are only interested in a God who will load them with 'health and wealth' through the so-called Word-Faith preachers of the prosperity gospel. Many of us have become lovers of pleasure more than lovers of God (2 Tim. 3:4). This is to our shame and puts us in spiritual jeopardy.

Even without the threat of the world tempting us to apostatise from Christ and instead pursue its material pleasures, as we have noted in a previous chapter, the greatest cause of the impotence of the Christian church these days is not necessarily the big sins, but simply that Christians are diverted by the trivia, by the infinite amount of time-wasting options, of the consumer society. Those things are perhaps not wrong in themselves. There may be nothing wrong with particular objects that we can buy, but it is just that our lives are cluttered and taken up with goods and services and entertainment and everything else that we can find time for. As that happens, our focus on 'You shall have no other gods but me' makes a quiet exit. Our Christian lives are vitiated, not necessarily by enormous corruptions, but trivial matters. In John Bunyan's words, we have been diverted into By-path Meadow. In old-fashioned language, we have become worldly.

Now Jesus wants to lead us out of that kind of captivity and to set before us a different vision. It is the exciting vision of the outcast who is also a revolutionary. It is the idea of one who is an outsider but nevertheless loves people and wants to transform culture and bring blessing to it. We are paradoxically against society for the good of society. So, with the current state of the Western evangelical church in mind, we look at these verses from Luke 6.

The Christian as outsider

First of all, we investigate verses 20-26, where we meet the Christian as an outsider. Those of us who are a little older may remember an individual who was prominent for a little while – Archbishop Makarios of Cyprus. He was a crucial figure in the politics of that country as it was striving to attain its independence back in the 1950s. His name actually means Archbishop 'Blessed'. *Makarios* is the Greek word for 'blessed' or 'happy'. In his book *Joy in the New Testament*, William G. Morrice tells us that in classical Greek, the form of this word used by Homer was, properly speaking, an epithet of the gods. In Plato, 'the blessed ones' are the more privileged classes – the rich and better educated people. 'By means of their wealth, they have been raised up out of the daily cares and distresses by which common people are troubled.'[1] Yet Jesus uses this word of the poor and ridiculed.

'Makarios' is the same word that we referred to in the last chapter, when we looked at Paul's description of the Lord as the ever-blessed God, the joyful, happy God, who wishes to share his joy with us. 'Makarios' are you who are poor – blessed, happy, fortunate, are you, says Jesus in verse 20. Here is the blessedness of God being predicated of certain people. Christianity is certainly not against people being happy. Christ wants people to find true joy, wholesome happiness, blessedness. Where is it found?

Blessings and woes

Here Jesus gives us four beatitudes, four 'blesseds':

'Blessed are you who are poor, for yours is the kingdom of God' (verse 20);

'Blessed are you who hunger now, for you will be satisfied';

'Blessed are you who weep now, for you will laugh' (verse 21);

'Blessed are you when men hate you, when they exclude you and insult you and reject your name as evil, because of the Son of Man' (verse 22).

Later he gives four woes:

'But woe to you who are rich, for you have already received your comfort (verse 24);

1. William G. Morrice, *Joy in the New Testament*, Paternoster, 1984, p. 44.

'Woe to you who are well fed now, for you will go hungry';

'Woe to you who laugh now, for you will mourn and weep' (verse 25);

'Woe to you when all men speak well of you, for that is how their fathers treated the false prophets' (verse 26).

The beatitudes do not confer blessing, they rather describe something that has already been conferred. They are equivalent of saying, 'Congratulations to you, because of this.' They describe the good fortune of a person. Similarly, the woes do not put a curse on people, but rather they lament the situation as it stands for that person.

Now these sayings of Jesus obviously contain a great paradox. 'Blessed are you who are poor', that doesn't sound right. How different from Plato's, and most other people's, view of blessedness. 'Woe to you who are rich and well-fed', that sounds a bit strange. The millions who buy their tickets for the national lottery would never agree with what Jesus says here. So how do we understand his words?

To use a technical word, we have to see that the blessings and the woes are *eschatological*, that is, they describe the present situation in the light of the ultimate future. Jesus emphasizes this for example in verse 21: 'You who hunger now, but (looking into the future) you will be satisfied'; or again, the other way round, in verse 25: 'Woe to you who are well-fed now, for you will (looking into the future) go hungry.' So these beatitudes and woes do not make an assessment on the basis of the present outward appearance of things. Instead, the Lord Jesus, the one uttering the blessing or woe, does so from a position within the counsels of God, with an awareness of the ultimate future.

I am reminded of the prophet Jeremiah's day. The false prophets were prophesying easy and comforting things for Judah and its people. They were just seeking popularity, endorsing the common wish of the people that all would be well, and dignifying those sentiments by the prefix 'Thus saith the LORD'. Their words were worse than useless. But Jeremiah, by the Spirit, had been into the counsel chamber of God and he could see what was going to happen. Jerusalem would be destroyed. From that vantage point he laments for the city: 'Woe to you, O Jerusalem! How long will you be unclean?' (Jer. 13:27). Of course, Jeremiah's predictions proved correct, for the Babylonian army sacked the great city. God's judgment had come.

Similarly it is from within the counsels of God, with an awareness of the ultimate outcome of history, that Jesus gives these blessings and these woes. 'Blessed are you who are poor, for yours is the kingdom of God.... Woe to you who are rich.' Jesus, the man who is God, is, to put it bluntly, viewing people in terms of heaven and hell, in terms of salvation or damnation.

Marks of grace

How, then, are we to understand these blessings and woes? Note the beginning of verse 20, because is crucial. It reads: 'Looking at his disciples, Jesus said: "Blessed are you who are poor." ' Jesus is not saying anything as simplistic as that all poor people inevitably go to heaven and all the rich go to hell. That is not what the Bible teaches. We must understand it in terms of Jesus looking at his disciples and saying, 'Blessed are *you.*' These men have left their jobs and income, some of them have left their families, and followed Jesus. What is being highlighted is this: something has happened to these people to make them true disciples. Something had happened in the hearts of these men to make them true followers, come what may, of Jesus Christ. And that thing had grasped them so deeply that they did not mind being poor or going hungry for Jesus' sake. They did not mind facing such troubles as made them weep or being outcasts in society for Jesus' sake, because their hopes of happiness, their expectancy of joy, was not rooted in this world, but in Christ and in God and in the world to come.

In that sense, although outwardly they are the same as everybody else on the face of the earth and they mix with people and seek to love people, inwardly the disciples of Jesus are different. If it doesn't sound too strange, we could say, inwardly they were outsiders. Their internal lives are different. Their hearts have been captivated by Christ. Their hopes are in the kingdom of God. 'Blessed are you who are poor, for yours is the kingdom of God.' Jesus is saying this: 'Blessed are you, you who are prepared to be poor and hungry, and whatever it takes to follow me, for that is the very mark that you really do belong to God and you are going to heaven. "Blessed are you" – what a fortunate person you are! Let me give a couple of examples of this.

Some of you may have read the missionary biography of John G. Paton from Dumfries in Scotland. In March 1858, he married Mary Ann Robson and in April they sailed together for the cannibal island of Tanna in the New Hebrides to take the gospel of the Lord Jesus to the inhabitants. In a little time they built a house, and Mary had given birth to a son within the first year of their marriage. Then on March 3, 1859, a year after their wedding, Mary died of fever and three weeks later her infant son died too. John Paton buried them alone, in unimaginable grief, far from friends and far from home. What sustained him in this terrible tragedy? He wrote: 'But for Jesus, I would have gone mad and died beside that lonely grave.' His hope was in Jesus. There were pressures upon him; his earthly joys, his wife and his child had gone. He was in effect saying, 'I would have gone mad had not my hope been somewhere else ultimately; my hope was in Jesus.' This is different from the people of the world. In the face of such tragedy many people would have cursed God with bitterness of heart, rather than finding solace in him. Paton was among those Jesus called blessed. And one of the gifts that the Lord had given him to sustain him in that time were words that his wife spoke shortly before her death. She did not murmur against God or resent her husband's missionary calling. Rather, she said, 'I do not regret leaving home and friends. If I had to do it again, I would do it with more pleasure, yes, with all my heart.' How could she say that? It was because her heart belonged to Jesus. Her heart was in the things of God. She was an outsider, different from this world. 'Blessed are you,' says Jesus. Do you see what is going on here? The source of their joy was Christ.

We can find another similar example in the apostle Paul's life. Remember how he puts it so vividly:

> But whatever was to my profit I now consider loss for the sake of Christ. What is more, I consider everything a loss compared to the surpassing greatness of knowing Christ Jesus my Lord, for whose sake I have lost all things. I consider them rubbish, that I may gain Christ and be found in him, not having a righteousness of my own

that comes from the law, but that which is through faith in Christ (Phil. 3:7-9).

Paul had moved among the upper classes of religious Judaism. He had friends, influence and a fine mind. The future, in worldly terms of prestige and power, was at his feet. But he spurned it all, for Christ's sake. Paul's heart is of the same kind as those of John Paton and his wife, isn't it? 'Blessed are you,' says Jesus, 'you weeping people who love me so much that you count the things of this world as nothing to follow me. Heaven is yours.'

But by contrast, in verses 24 and 25: 'Woe to you who are rich, for you have already received your comfort.' 'Woe to you who are well-fed now, for you will go hungry.' 'Woe to you who laugh now, for you will mourn and weep.' There are those whose delights and enjoyment are only in this world. Their riches mean that they are never at a loss to be entertained, never at a loss to be stroked and comforted, never at a loss to be as full and content as they are. They can always afford to go to see some new place or buy some new thing to cheer themselves up. Such 'retail therapy' is a way of life for them. The wealthy can always be distracted. But that means they rarely if ever give a thought to eternity and so they are lost. They never take seriously God and the claims of Christ, and their continual diversions lead them to damnation. 'Woe to you, I lament for you,' says Jesus.

Heaven and hell for consumers

It is instructive to note the underlying pictures here of heaven and hell. They are very relevant to a consumer society. The underlying pictures are in terms of eternal gain and eternal loss. There is the eternal reward, laughter and satisfaction (verse 21) for those who belong to Christ, whose hearts are his. There is the eternal hunger, weeping and loss, eternal gnawing emptiness (verse 25) for those who have set their hopes on this world and have nothing in Christ. Those who are satisfied with this world and its pleasures reject God, they do not want him. Therefore, hell is very just. In one sense hell is simply God withdrawing himself and all his goodness and his forbearance. In a sense he is giving these people what they always wanted. They have refused the voice of God in their consciences, they are not interested in the presence of God in Christ, and now he is gone forever. By contrast, heaven is God giving himself to those whose hearts have been changed and have come to absolutely delight in him and love him. God says, 'I give myself and my kingdom to you for your continual pleasure and rejoicing in me, and to have fellowship with me.'

Heaven is a wonderful place. No-one will ever be bored in heaven. In heaven all things are made new. It is often a desire for 'newness' which drives the consumer to go and acquire new things all the time. The cut of the new dress or the smell of the brand new car is so seductive. But only in God do we find what souls are really looking for in this desire for the 'new thing'. Through Christ's new covenant we have new birth, we have new hearts, we are given a new name, we live by a new commandment, we sing a new song of praise to God, and we will dwell in a new Jerusalem in a new heaven and new earth (Heb. 12:24; 1 Pet. 1:3; Ezek. 36:26; Isa. 62:2; John 13:34; Rev. 5:9; 21:1,2). Jonathan Edwards writes this: 'In heaven, 'tis the directly reverse of what 'tis on earth, for there by length of time, things become more and more youthful.' On earth as time progresses everything becomes older, and decays (it is the second law of thermodynamics!). But in heaven the longer we are there everything is more and more vigorous, active, tender and beautiful. Those whose happiness is in the riches and goods of this life have a treasure which will only decrease. But the true Christian has an inheritance that can never diminish or fade.

The Scriptures are not condemning people who are rich, but they are saying if that is where your heart is, 'Woe to you.' If you are a Christian and you have money and you use it for the Lord, your heart belongs to him. The state of your heart is shown by the way that you actually use money to praise God. But those whose happiness is this world, and that is what the consumer society holds out to us all the time, have a treasure that can only decrease and will end in everlasting emptiness.

A new way of seeing

There are two things that we need to conclude from this first section of the chapter. The first is that it brings us back again to reconsidering the way we look at the world. What is your attitude to the world? Are you taken in by its outward representation?

The consumer society is a society which is based on outward image. What matters is how things look. What the customer sees is so important. It is what sells the article. But outward image is not how Jesus is assessing the world. Can you see that it looks good? Can you see that it looks rich? Can you have it now? Can you touch it and taste it?

That is how the consumer society is telling us to assess everything. But Jesus says: 'No, it may look good now, but I am telling you to see things in terms of the eternal future.' As we move through this world, in the consumer culture, bear in mind the way that Jesus viewed the world. He is the Son of God, his vision of the world is spiritual 20-20 vision. He sees it precisely as it is. To view the world in any other way is to be led astray. That is the first thing we need to grasp.

The great change

Secondly, I must ask every reader the big question. With the disciples, something had changed their hearts, so they didn't mind being poor for Jesus, or weeping for Jesus' sake. The great question I must ask you is: Has that great change happened to you? The old hymn says:

> I would rather have Jesus than silver or gold,
> I'd rather be his than have riches untold;
> I'd rather have Jesus than houses or lands,
> I'd rather be led by his nail pierced hands
> Than to be the king of a vast domain
> and be held in sin's dread sway;
> I'd rather have Jesus than anything
> this world affords today.

Has that great change happened to you? If you have truly been converted, you have had an experience like that of the Prodigal Son. You know the time when you went your own way and you ended up filling your life with the things of this world which leave you empty. You had your belly-full with what the pigs would feed on. It dawned upon you somehow, as it did with that Prodigal Son, that there was something much better: 'There is a Father who loves me, there is a Father who has a house which is all delights and for whom my heart was made.' You came to your senses and saw through the things of this world, and said: 'I will rise and go to my father. I will go without delay. I will confess my sin and corruption and I will cast myself upon his mercy in Jesus. And I will do that no matter what I lose. *I will do it come what may*!'

Has that change happened to you? So that you can truly say: 'Whatever people take away from me, I cling to Jesus.' If you have, then Christ says to you, 'Blessed are you, happy are you, to be congratulated are you, for yours is the kingdom of God.' That is the mark of salvation.

If you have not come to him, I plead with you to do so.

The Christian as revolutionary

Now, when the great change takes place within us, we often find ourselves out of step with society. Jesus highlights that in verses 22 and 23. Sometimes we can find ourselves out of step with our families if they are not Christian. Sometimes we can find ourselves rejected, cold-shouldered, by people at work. They feel, as we have seen, that to some extent we are outsiders to them. The things they take delight in no longer interest us in the same way as they interest them. Frequently they are affronted by this. Their obsessions, and what they call so precious, we treat as if they are only secondary matters. Things that they are giving all their lives for, we are saying, are insignificant in the long run. The matters we want to talk about, to challenge them, they don't want to talk about. So we feel ourselves as outsiders, and they feel as if we are outsiders.

When that happens to us, how are we to react? Well, we are told in verses 27-36. Jesus said: 'But I tell you who hear me. Love your enemies, do good to those who hate you, bless those who curse you, pray for those who ill-treat you.' The Christian, if we take Jesus' agenda seriously, is not only someone who is an outsider in this world, but the Christian is also someone who is called to lovingly subvert and undermine the system of this world. That is why I have given this section the title of 'The Christian as revolutionary'.

We are called to be revolutionaries and it shows: 'Love your enemies...' (verse 27); 'Give to everyone who asks you, and if anyone takes what belongs to you, do not demand it back' (verse 30); 'If you love those who love you, what credit is that to you? Even "sinners" love those who love them' (verse 32). The system of relationships in this world, we could give it the name of 'reciprocity'. It is like a commercial arrangement, what the consumer society would call fair exchange: 'Because you have given me something, I will give you something equal in return.' It is the way of comparable return. That is how the world works. But how do we respond when people are nasty to us? Well, the normal way of the world would be, if someone strikes you, you have every reason to give him a black eye in return. But to the Christian Jesus says, 'Be different. Be subversive. If someone strikes you on one cheek, turn to him the other also. If someone takes your cloak, do not stop him from taking your coat.' We are to do to others, not what the world expects us to do, but what we would like done to us if we were in their shoes.

I would say this humbly to everyone who belongs to a

church: please be careful how you treat one another. Don't fall into treating each other in the church the way that the world treats one another. If someone rubs you up the wrong way, perhaps you don't speak to them again or else you avoid them. That is the way of the world. Please take seriously what Christ is saying. No matter what they have done, he is calling us to a different kind of life, to be a different kind of community, subversive of the world.

The positive side of the world's way of doing things is what you might call market exchange. We love those who love us and do good to those who do good to us (verse 33). If you do that, what credit is that to you? There is nothing wrong with it, but there is nothing distinctively Christian about it. That is the way that the world operates. You are not only called to do that, you are called to be a revolutionary, to be a subversive. Therefore, 'love your enemies, do good to them, and lend to them without expecting to get anything back. Then your reward will be great and you will be sons of the Most High' (verse 35). Jesus is again telling us to see the relationships of this world in terms of the eternal future.

Reasons for the revolution

I want to suggest two reasons as to why Jesus is calling us to this kind of action, this kind of revolutionary lifestyle.

First of all, there is the reason given in the passage. We are to live and love differently from the world, in order to direct the world to the grace of God. How does ordinary Joe Bloggs think of God and of going to heaven? He thinks he has to be good enough. He thinks that if God is there at all, he is a heavenly headmaster for whom you must pass an exam. He thinks that he can earn points by being good and then God will sit down one day and tot up the marks and say: 'Well, has he or hasn't he? No, he has not got there' or 'Yes, he has, I'll let him into my heaven.' That is how the natural man thinks. He thinks that heaven is a matter of merit. But that is completely wrong. No-one will gain heaven by merit. We have all sinned and fallen so dreadfully far short of the glory of God that there is nothing we can do to save ourselves.

But the Most High is kind to the ungrateful and the wicked. It is a wonder of wonders that while we were still sinners, Christ died for the ungodly, and that all who come to him and put their trust in him will be saved. The way to heaven is through God's mercy. Now in order to set people on the right track we are to live life in a way that is filled with the grace and mercy of God – and that is subversive of the world's way. We must live differently. People do not have to pass our exam of being 'nice' or 'deserving' in order for us to do good to them. We are to act out of pure mercy. This will provide the context in which we can teach them of the grace of God in the gospel. They are to be able to see the evidence of the grace of God in our lives and in the church (Acts 11:23). That is the first reason we are to live as revolutionaries.

John Wesley's problem

The second reason is perhaps rather different. It is not in the passage, but it seems to me that we need to take this on board. I want to suggest that there may be another extremely important reason why Christians must live with the subversive generosity of which Jesus speaks.

You see, without generosity, Christianity has a real problem at a very practical level. I realize that those of you who are in business will have to think this thing through very carefully, more carefully than I am bringing it to you in this book. But it was indeed a very insightful man, John Wesley, who saw this problem. The problem he saw is in the Protestant work ethic. He saw, rightly, that the New Testament calls Christians to honesty, to hard work and to be productive people. That is absolutely true, that is what we are called to be if we are called to be Christians. If we look at passages such as Ephesians 6:5-9; Colossians 3:22-25; 2 Thessalonians 3:6-15 we would see this. But Wesley worried in this way about Christianity:

> Christianity (if it is taken seriously) must necessarily produce both industry and frugality and therefore cannot but produce riches, but as riches increase [it is the proven track record as it were, he was saying] so will pride, anger and love of the world in all its branches. [Brackets mine.]

Do you see what he is saying? There is nothing wrong with productiveness and honesty and hard work. That is right, that is what we are called to. But on its own it cannot but inevitably make Christians comparatively rich people in the long term. Then riches tend to undermine our spirituality. That is the problem, he says. Christians should work hard and yet, he says, 'wherever riches have increased, the essence of religion has decreased in the same proportion.'

It seems to me that this is the reason why historically evangelicalism can so easily slide in a generation or two into secularism. Yes, grandma and granddad believed that.

But we have made our way in the world, we are rich now and all that is behind us and we do not need God. We are happy without him. We are secular now. The things of this world have taken over the family. This kind of scenario has repeated itself often throughout history, from the days of ancient Israel down to the present time.

Perhaps we could see in broad brush strokes the whole history of the United States in the same way. Good and godly men and women left Europe to find a new world where they could practise their biblical faith without hindrance. The founding fathers were great men. Then the powerful influence of the Protestant work ethic generated the hard-working American attitude which brought tremendous success to that land rich in resources. But as America became the land of plenty, so true religion has degenerated there. Yes, many people still call themselves Christian and attend church, but much of it is empty, and there has arisen in the United States the most virulent forms of secular lifestyle. Satisfied with riches, you can so easily forget God.

What is the answer? Jesus said, 'Give to everyone who asks you, and if anyone takes what belongs to you, do not demand it again. Love your enemies and do good to them, lend to them without expecting to get anything back, then your reward will be great.' As I said, this needs to be thought through very carefully, but so often Christians have treated generosity as a kind of 'added extra' to their Christian lives. It is not. It is essential for the glory of God and it is essential for the health of our own spirituality. We are to be givers rather than buyers. We are to be Christlike rather than consumers. Where Christians are not generous givers true faith inevitably degenerates. Sadly, that is the process which the church in the Western world is locked into, by and large, at the present time. We need to wake up and seek again the Christian counter-culture.

As Christians, then, we are called in the words of O'Shaunnessy's poem to be world losers and world forsakers, dreamers of dreams that this world cannot understand. As we take those things seriously, the vision of Christ will become a reality. We will become movers and shakers. We will change society in the right direction, towards God's kingdom.

CHAPTER 4

THE MIGHTY MEDIA

1953 was the year television broke through in Britain. Why was that? It was the year of the coronation of Queen Elisabeth II. In post-war patriotic Britain this was an event of huge public interest. Not many people had TVs up until then, but when they realised that with a television set they could see the Queen crowned in their own front-room, great numbers of the population bought televisions. That was the big step forward. Suddenly there was a major audience looking to see 'what's on telly?'

Since then the TV has in many ways conquered the world. We now live in a media age dominated by film and TV. Figures for 1993 showed that the average British person is in front of the television screen for between 15 and 20-plus hours a week. This is quite a long time. It is almost a whole day in front of the screen. With such exposure TV (and also the cinema) shapes people's thinking, in many ways it now moulds the whole of society. The way people run politics, sport, education and much more is all geared to TV coverage. Society is increasingly shaped by this great new phenomenon which has come upon the world at the end of the twentieth century.

We are trying to think through what is required by way of being a disciple of Christ in a consumer culture. We have defined consumerism along these kinds of lines: consumerism is a promise of happiness through material goods and services which, in particular, massages the thrill that we get from the power of personal choice. It makes us a little bit like a god, to be able to choose what we will have. There is nothing wrong with happiness, there is nothing wrong with the material world, but consumerism calls us to find our joy in the world. Our happiness is found not in God our Creator, but in created things and our control of them.

At the risk of stating the obvious, it is clear that there is a close alliance between TV and consumerism. Not only are we bombarded with advertising and selling from the commercial screen, but TV ravishes our eyes with the sights of the material world – all kinds of places that we can be taken to, all kinds of things we can experience. Furthermore, with the proliferation of satellite and cable stations, the TV manufacturers give you the remote control channel-changer; they put it into your hand and say: 'Sit there and choose!' TV is a visual/material world. And it is about choice, so it is alive with the whole idea of consumerism. There is a *symbiotic* relationship between the TV and consumerism – they feed off each other.

An analysis of TV

So the first thing I want to do is to try to give an analysis of TV and film and the ideas and forces behind them.

But before we get going, I want to say this: there are many things on TV which are fine and wholesome. There are innocent quiz shows which test the mind. There are programmes which educate us and expand our understanding. There are classic drama series which bring Charles Dickens' or Jane Austen's novels to the screen. These are good. I need to say that because overall I am going to give a negative view and I want to try to keep a balance. There are some fine, noble programmes on TV.

But it seems to me that we need to look beneath the programming, we need to look below into the nature of TV itself. Back in the 1960s, Marshall McLuhan (1911-1980), the Canadian theorist of communication, became famous through a particular slogan. He was a commentator on the effects of technology on society and his slogan was this: 'The medium is the message.' What he was saying is that the way a message is communicated to us is a message in itself. The way a message comes to us is saying something in itself.

This is profound, but not too profound. We know this just from ordinary life. We can say the same words in different tones of voice and mean completely different things. Take the words, 'Oh yes.' One usage indicates a person is listening to what another says. Another usage questions what has just been said. A third usage is seen in a person on the terraces at the football match leaping up and shouting, 'Oh yes!'; he is not asking a question, he is making a statement that a goal has been scored, or whatever. The message is completely different, simply through the tone of voice that is used. The tone of voice is the medium in which the message is coming to us and, as our examples show, the medium itself can very much shape the message and is a message in and of itself.

If the medium is the message, then by the very fact of what TV is, there are subtle messages inherent in it of which we need to be aware. There are subtle ideas conveyed to us simply through the fact of what TV is. I am going to try and analyse it under five headings which make up the acronym VIDEO.

The world of the Visual

First of all, when we come to TV, we come to the world of the visual. It sounds obvious, but TV and films heavily rely on the visual to communicate and in that there is a hidden message. The message inherent in TV and film is 'what you see is what is true'. Or to put it another way, 'what you see is what you can believe'. That is the kind of message that is right there in the way that it is coming to us.

For ordinary secular folk that might sound spot on. The idea that 'seeing is believing' is their very creed. In many ways we can go along with it. Our eyes are an enormous help in living life. Blind people have immense problems. But let me put it another way: the message of TV is that 'the apparent is the actual'. Immediately we hear it put like that, you think: 'Hold on, is that right? Is the apparent total reality?' We can think of master illusionists. We can think of the Nazi propaganda machine. Such manipulations of the visual should be enough to make any person hesitate. Christians in particular should say that it isn't right at all. Why? Because the Bible divides everything into two categories: the Creator who rules and the creation that he has made.

The Creator who has made all things is invisible. Exodus 20:3,4 reads: 'You shall have no other gods before me.... You shall not make for yourself an idol in the form of anything.' Because God is invisible, we cannot make a representation of him because we cannot see him. Again, in Isaiah 46:5 the Lord asks one of his great questions: 'To whom will you compare me or count me equal? To whom will you liken me?' Is there some person, some image, some object, that we can say that God is like? Well, there isn't, because he is totally different. So that is one reason why Christians immediately should say, 'Hold on' when we think about the TV message that what you see is what is true.

Again, we know that this subtle message is not a totally reliable statement from our everyday lives. We can be misled by people's words and behaviour. People can tell lies. We cannot see into their motives and purposes. We can misunderstand people. Remember when the prophet Samuel went to the house of Jesse to anoint a new king. God had told him to anoint one of the sons of Jesse. Samuel saw several strapping young men, but regarding each one God said to the prophet, 'It is not him.' Rather, God said, 'Man looks at the outward appearance but the LORD looks at the heart' (1 Sam. 16:7). The one whom God had chosen was young David. He did not look much, but God knew his heart. Similarly, TV is not the truth. It is half truth. It pretends to be the whole truth but the visual cannot be so easily trusted.

Indeed, surely the idea that what you see is what you can believe was actually contributory to the original Fall of mankind in the Garden of Eden. If you look at Genesis 2 and 3 you find there a tension between the word of God, the command that had been spoken, and the delicious look of the forbidden fruit. Prompted by Satan's sowing of doubt in her mind Eve stands at a crossroads. Would she trust the visual appearance of the fruit or what God had said? In 2:17, God said: 'you must not eat from the tree of the knowledge of good and evil, for when you eat of it, you will surely die.' In 3:6, the text says: 'When the woman saw that the fruit of the tree was good and pleasing to the eye, and also desirable for gaining wisdom, she took some and ate it.' Because she doubted God's word there was a tension between the unseen word of God and the seeming evidence of her own eyes. The tension there underlines to us again that the idea that seeing is believing cannot be totally relied upon. It is not a biblical perspective and is something to be questioned carefully.

The world of the Instant

The second thing concerning TV is that we come to the world of the instant. Everything is immediate. Film and TV concentrate on the faculty of sight. Naturally, the only thing we can see is this instant. All you can see is right now. You can't, with your eyes, see yesterday or two years in the future. All you can see is this moment. You can remember yesterday but memory is not your eyes. Sight is a 'now' faculty. So TV has a second hidden message: it is subtly telling you that now is the only time that really matters.

This means that television has a very subtle way of disengaging us from the past. To many modern youngsters in school, history is boring because it's not on film. Because most of it is not in moving pictures they don't take much notice. Of course, you might have films about the future, but it doesn't make you think in terms of the future. It feels as if you are in the future now. It disengages us from a broader time perspective and makes us focus on this instant. It tells our subconscious that what matters is simply now. And if we let our children drink in TV all the time, their attitude for life will be that now is all that really matters.

But, although now is very important, to be totally focused on now is something which the Bible would warn against. Now is important, now is the day of salvation. Now you have the opportunity to serve God, to turn to God. But to think only in terms of now would be in fact to undermine the Bible's message. The apostle John writes:

> Do not love the world or anything in the world. If anyone loves the world, the love of the Father is not in him. For everything in the world – the cravings of sinful man, the lust of his eyes and the boasting of what he has and does – comes not from the Father but from the world. The world and its desires pass away, but the man who does the will of God lives for ever (1 John 2:15-17).

Things that are now are temporary, says the Scripture. You can only understand now properly in the light of eternity; in the light of the things that you cannot visualise, that you cannot put on film, the things of God.

We lament the moral decline of society in the West. It seems to me that this kind of pressurized 'now' emphasis is, in many ways, what makes the world-view put over by TV something that erodes morality. There are no consequences, there is simply now. There is no Judgment Day that you have to think about, it is just now. When TV is 'good' it engrosses people completely in what they are viewing. TV captivates people's attention, so that often there is no time to reflect on what is being seen. This reinforces the message that it is only now that matters. We will come back to this. But you see how TV subverts people's way of thinking about life.

The world of the Distant

The third observation that I will make about TV is that it is also the world of the distant. Pictures come to us from far away through the TV. Yet though the TV is immediate and instant, there is also a sense of distance. So, for example, we could cope with watching the pictures of the famine in Ethiopia in the 1980s because we were distant from it. We could watch the pictures of the war-torn streets in Bosnia in the early 1990s because we were distant from it. We were not actually involved in the famine, we were not going to get caught in the crossfire. We were at a distance from these things even though they were going on, as it were, right now. This blunts our moral sensibilities. We can see terrible things, but it does not endanger us. We can see terrible violence but it is 'only acting'.

So another subtle message from watching from a distance is that these tragedies cannot hurt us and morality does not matter too much. But the Christian must pause, for such an idea is not true. What we see can affect us greatly, therefore we need to be careful about what we allow ourselves to see. Jesus said in Matthew 6:22: 'The eye is the lamp of the body. If your eyes are good, your whole body will be full of light. But if your eyes are bad, your whole body will be full of darkness. If then the light within you is darkness, how great is that darkness!' I know this verse has a spiritual meaning, but it also has a straightforward meaning. If we allow our sight to be filled with things that are corrupt and godless, it will affect us deep inside. We need to be careful.

The world of the Entertaining

Fourthly, TV is the world of the entertaining. The TV image has to be entertaining, it has to make itself more interesting than the sitting room wallpaper, otherwise you would look at the wallpaper rather than the TV screen! So it has to take its material and show it in a way that fascinates, and excites, and interests. But with this pressure to entertain, what tends to happen is that whatever TV touches, it trivialises.

If we think about politics we realize that important issues are being addressed. Decisions will be taken which chart the economic, legal and social welfare of the nation. People's jobs and their futures hang on the direction of a Government decision. Yet when politics is handled on TV it more often than not comes down to a sound-bite and a photo opportunity. Some would say it has been reduced to a beauty competition. That is how politics is conducted in the television age. The real arguments are often bypassed. Extended, careful thought is 'boring'.

TV has to capture our attention. It does that, not only by using beautiful presenters and gifted, talented people, but, in particular, it captures our attention by repeatedly changing the image so that there is always something new. Neil Postman, in his book, *Amusing Ourselves to Death*, says that the average length of the shot on network TV in America is only 3.5 seconds, so that the eye never rests and always has something new to see. All the time the camera angle is changing, all the time there is something different. We zoom in, we pull out again, someone else comes on. There is something new, all the time. Now, not only does that probably diminish many people's concentration spans (if we wonder why young children have difficulty learning in school when they have been stuck in front of the television for so many years, it is because they are just not used to concentrating that long any more), but it also has an inbuilt message about entertainment. The message in TV is that unless something is moving visually, it's boring. Unless something is entertaining, it is not worth paying attention to. People have been trained by continually watching TV to always expect things to be entertaining.

But the Bible tells us that not everything worthwhile is entertaining. It is a mistake to equate what is valuable with what is exciting. Things that are real and have to be dealt with cannot always be made entertaining. In Ezekiel 33, God berated the people of Israel for treating the prophet and the preacher as if he was just a piece of show business. In verses 30-32 he says:

> As for you, son of man, your countrymen are talking together about you by the walls and at the doors of the houses, saying to each other, 'Come and hear the message that has come from the LORD.' My people come to you, as they usually do, and sit before you to listen to your words, but they do not put them into practice. With their mouths they express devotion, but their hearts are greedy for unjust gain. Indeed, to them you are nothing more than one who sings love songs with a beautiful voice and plays an instrument well, for they hear your words but do not put them into practice.

Some things are too serious to be treated as show business. There is a place for entertainment in our lives, but we cannot make everything into entertainment. It is a complete perversion of the world and indeed brings the displeasure of God.

Let me again point out one other matter under this

heading. TV is capable of throwing so many images, so much information, at us in a small amount of time that our minds are incapable of reflecting properly on all we are given. TV is not like a book. It does not let us stop and pause for thought. Unless what we are watching is on video, there is no way to stop the flow and come back to it later. It keeps rolling. We cannot think through everything that is communicated to us in such a short space of time.

One common reaction, therefore, as we noted in chapter 2, is that TV encourages people not to think, but to make decisions simply on their feelings. We cannot think all this through because it is just too complicated. All these little sound-bites are part of a much more complicated reality which is just too vast for us to grasp. So how are we going to make a decision about what we are being told by the TV? Our minds cannot cope, so we go to our emotions. That is more simple. So now we only ask, 'How does it make me feel? Good or bad? Good. OK, that's the one I'll choose.'

Think of this way of response in relation to politics. Don't worry about the issues or the consequences of policies; whatever argument someone comes up with, someone else can come up with a counter-argument. We have not the time on television to have all the facts and all the information before us. So we end up with: 'Who looks nice? Who says "trust me" and looks fairly sincere? Let's vote for him.' That is what it comes down to.

But it is dangerous. Living on feelings is not the way for a Christian life to develop. 'Therefore, I urge you, brothers, in view of God's mercy, to offer your bodies as living sacrifices, holy and pleasing to God – which is your spiritual act of worship. Do not conform any longer to the pattern of this world, but be transformed by the renewing of your mind' (Rom. 12:1,2). Not feelings, but the mind, and the attitude of your mind, is the key to Christian discipleship. Beware the 'feel good' factor pushed by the TV world of entertainment.

The world of the Optional

Fifthly, regarding the world of TV, we come to the world of the optional. Years ago, when I was a youngster, TV used to be something of a unifying influence in the nation. There were only two channels you could watch, BBC and ITV. We had all watched *Tony Hancock's Half-hour* the day before, so we could all talk about it at school. It was something that brought people together in some way. Those days have gone. Now there are so many channels, and along with the advent of video, the choice of viewing is enormous. If you have a hobby, there are TV channels devoted to your interest. There are sports channels, discovery channels, movie channels. If you are from an alternative lifestyle or a particular ethnic background, there is another channel for you to do your viewing. The variety of possible viewing actually isolates people away from each other. It causes people to turn their backs on being part of the whole community.

At a Christian convention not too long ago I heard an excellent talk by Elaine Storkey, of the London Institute for Contemporary Christianity, on this matter of the media. She was speaking about the TV soap operas. She spoke about how very often they are written to a formula. As human beings, made in the image of the triune God, we have a need for relationships with others. So in soap operas, you will find that there is always a spectrum of different characters. There is the careful one, the wayward one, the honest one, the sly one, the one who is an extrovert, the one who is an introvert, and so on. All these are built into the plot.

They are planted there for a reason. It is so that you, whoever you are, will be able to find someone in the programme who is a bit like you and to whom you can relate. That is the first thing.

Second, within that spectrum of characters, you can find others, in a way, to interact with. These are people that you will judge and criticise and weigh up or whom you are going to be sympathetic towards. Now what happens? Something like this: here are a lot of people that you can interact with and who speak to something of that need you have for relationships. But, at the same time, they are a lot easier to deal with than people in the real world. They are easier to deal with than real people because the TV characters are not going to make any demands of you. If you don't like them, you can turn them off or just turn to another soap opera that you may like a bit better. Put bluntly, we begin to be influenced by feeling 'who needs relationships with real people because this is much easier to handle?' Especially if we have had a tough time from real people, we can shut the front door and live within our TV world. Whereas people used to interact with neighbours, colleagues and friends, our society these days is becoming more and more isolated. The TV society, hooked on taking easy options, is becoming a fragmented and lonely society. Whereas God's Word tells us to love our neighbour as ourselves, the TV tempts us to close the door and live in a private fantasy world.

I am putting all the negatives and I realise that. I said at the beginning of the chapter that there are positives. But I am putting all the negatives because we need to be forced to think carefully about TV. The degree to which the fantasy world of TV influences us can be seen in the tabloid newspapers which no longer actually report real news. The major events of world affairs are often totally missing from their front pages. Instead there are stories about television soap stars in real life as if they were actually the characters they play on TV. It is weird, it isn't real, and yet people buy it. The influence of the media on our culture is a not a small thing.

What to do?

Let me make two practical applications. The first has to do with our use of TV. Remember, we are thinking about consumerism. Here is a summary of the inherent messages of TV:

What you see is what is true.
What is now is what really matters.
What is only on a screen cannot hurt you.
What is entertaining is what is good.
What you choose is what is best.

Put all that together and what do we get? Can you see that if consumerism is the prevalent secular ideology, TV is its prophet. TV is taking the ideology of the secular 'gospel' and saying to you: 'This is the way to live.' What you see is what is true. What is now is what really matters. Morality doesn't matter too much. What is entertaining is what is good. What you choose is what is best. As Christians we may think that the only time we are on the receiving end of preaching is for an hour or so in church on a Sunday. That is wrong. There is a sense in which we receive secular preaching every time we switch on the TV. There are good things being screened, but there is also a lot of godless propaganda. But no matter what a programme's content, a subtle message is being expounded to us. We need to know what we are handling.

Obviously we should not watch anything pornographic or viciously violent. These things are immoral and wrong in God's sight (Phil. 4:8). But we should also realise that we are up against something which is inherently secular in the way it is coming to us. We come to church to learn about how to live as Christians. Similarly, there is a real sense, at a low level, that every time we turn on the TV, we are being subtly trained to live as a secular consumer.

Some Christians will come to the conclusion that because TV is so bad, there should be total abstinence from it. We need to respect that view. Others will say that there are some good things, so we need to be careful about what we watch. I am not saying that everyone should throw away their TVs. But we must understand how it affects us.

The importance of Jesus
The second practical application is for us to recognise again the importance of the Lord Jesus and the Scriptures.

We have looked at the way TV pretends to be the truth, but is in fact at best half truth. So where do we see the truth? The answer is, in the Scriptures and Jesus Christ. The great emphasis in the New Testament is that faith in Christ enables us to see what is beyond sight. It brings us the truth we cannot see with our physical eyes or the TV camera. Hebrews 11 makes this emphasis: 'Faith is being sure of what we hope for and certain of what we do not see' (verse 1); 'By faith Noah, when warned about things not yet seen' (verse 7); Moses 'persevered because he saw him who is invisible' (verse 27).

Each Christian has been given that faculty of faith. In that sense each has the ability to see what other people cannot see. We can see the invisible. By faith we see God. What a wonderful faculty we have been given. We have been given the power of the Holy Spirit in order to actually perceive who Jesus is, to see something of God by faith. That makes the Lord Jesus very, very important.

The theologian, Jacques Ellul, wrote this about Jesus:

> The incarnation is the only moment in world history when truth rejoined appearances, when it completely penetrates appearances and changes them at their roots. The incarnation is the point where appearance ceases to be a diversion from truth and where truth ceases being the fatal judgment on appearances. At this moment, the Word can be seen. The Word became flesh. Sight can be believed because in the incarnation, but only there, sight is related to truth. The image which normally does not have the force of truth becomes proved when the image is Jesus Christ who is the image of the living God.[1]

We cannot equate appearances with truth. In a visually dominated age, everyone wants everything in terms of sight. The Christian is called to something rather different. Not

1. Jacques Ellul, *The Humiliation of the Word*, Eerdmans.

that we do not use our God-given faculty of sight; of course we do, but we use it with a little question mark over it, knowing that Jesus Christ is the true truth. He is reality.

In a visually dominated age, the battle for truth sometimes has to involve denying that ultimate truth can be seen. Where then do we find the truth? Today, we do not see Jesus with our eyes. We find him and his truth in the Word of God, written by those who had the tremendous privilege of being eye-witnesses of Jesus Christ.

How much time do we spend with our Bibles and how much time do we spend with the TV? It is a challenge.

CHAPTER 5

CONSUMERISM AND PERSONAL IDENTITY

Please read Luke 10:25-37

[25]On one occasion an expert in the law stood up to test Jesus. 'Teacher,' he asked, 'what must I do to inherit eternal life?'

[26]'What is written in the Law?' he replied. 'How do you read it?'

[27]He answered: ' "Love the Lord your God with all your heart and with all your soul and with all your strength and with all your mind"; and, "Love your neighbor as yourself." '

[28]'You have answered correctly,' Jesus replied. 'Do this and you will live.'

[29]But he wanted to justify himself, so he asked Jesus, 'And who is my neighbor?'

[30]In reply Jesus said: 'A man was going down from Jerusalem to Jericho, when he fell into the hands of robbers. They stripped him of his clothes, beat him and went away, leaving him half dead. [31]A priest happened to be going down the same road, and when he saw the man, he passed by on the other side. [32]So too, a Levite, when he came to the place and saw him, passed by on the other side. [33]But a Samaritan, as he traveled, came where the man was; and when he saw him, he took pity on him. [34]He went to him and bandaged his wounds, pouring on oil and wine. Then

he put the man on his own donkey, took him to an inn and took care of him. [35]The next day he took out two silver coins and gave them to the innkeeper. "Look after him," he said, "and when I return, I will reimburse you for any extra expense you may have."

[36]'Which of these three do you think was a neighbor to the man who fell into the hands of robbers?'

[37]The expert in the law replied, 'The one who had mercy on him.'

Jesus told him, 'Go and do likewise.'

During the forty-year period before the Berlin Wall came down in 1989, West German car manufacturing developed wonderfully in quality. We now see all the marvellous BMWs and Volkswagens on our roads. But during the same period in Communist East Germany, the car industry stood still. They were still making the same models of cars in 1989 that they made in the 1950s.

Technology did not change in the East because there was no market in the communist state. There was no consumer power to force manufacturers to improve what they produced. So we can see that, in some ways, a market has good effects. It pushes the manufacturers to be ever seeking to improve their product.

The ever-changing society

We are thinking about living as Christians in a consumer society. What we can notice from the example of the two Germanys is that a consumer society will be a dynamic society, a changing society. It is ever on the move. It is never static, everything is pushed towards progress. There is more choice, there are more rights and better products. All the time there is change. The reason we need to pick up on this is because living in that kind of ever-changing culture actually changes the way people see themselves. Their self-understanding is influenced by the perpetual motion of their environment. To a certain extent that rubs off on us as Christians as well. It changes the way people see themselves and therefore the way they tend to run their lives.

What do we mean? Time was when people chose and behaved according to who they were. Their identity was defined by various issues like social class, race or religion. Their choices were a function of their social class, or their gender, or their occupation, or their ethnic background, or their religion. To give you a simple example: I grew up among working-class people. Back in the 1950s, working-class people did not drink wine – that was the middle-class thing to do. The working-class person drank beer because that was to be working-class. In the same era, regarding holidays, ordinary folk went to certain places in the country and those higher up the strata of society went elsewhere, often abroad. Obviously these choices had a lot to do with the amount of money people earned, but that too was linked to social class. The choices were geared into your background, to who you were. People chose and acted according to their identity.

That mindset had its problems, but it did have a positive side. It meant that you knew who you were, and therefore you knew basically the direction in which you were going in life. If you were a Christian, you knew what kind of lifestyle was expected of you. It was clear. But nowadays, although there is still a link between the choices people make and their identity, in a consumer society the direction of that link is being reversed. Instead of people choosing according to who they are, now in a consumer society you can choose to a large extent who you want to be. You can choose your identity.

In a society where everything is constantly changing and everything can be bought, you can shop around for a new identity. You can buy into a different lifestyle for a little while, and when you have had enough of that, you can buy a new one. All you have to do is pay for the appropriate status symbols. You can be whoever you want to be. You do not need to feel trapped as a working-class man or a middle-class woman. Identity is an optional matter, just buy the clothes and change your image. You can be more than one person at the same time if you want to. You can be one kind of person when you are out with your friends and another kind of person when you are at work. That is perfectly acceptable now. That is the way things have changed.

Image and identity

But because such consumer identity is merely another consumer item which you can throw away at any time, two things happen. First of all, the idea of identity is *devalued*. It is not really a true identity that you buy, it is just a mask that you put on. That is one of the reasons why today so many people actually do not know who they are. They are lost because they just change from one idea of what their life should be and who they are, to another.

Eventually they find themselves without any certainties in life, all at sea without an anchor. It devalues and confuses personal identity (issues of self-acceptance and self-worth come in here too).

But secondly, what happens is that because it's only an image, people don't take too seriously any moral or ethical demands which might be made by taking on a new image. A new identity is not seen to have much permanence. Obligations and commitments which used to attach to a person's position or persona in life are now taken less seriously. A person's public office is seen as totally divorced from the goings on of their private life. Hypocrisy is not regarded in the same way as it was a generation ago. Public and private identities have nothing to do with each other. And such attitudes, especially among the young, largely vitiate the concept of Christian conversion. It weakens that link between how we see ourselves and how we feel we ought to behave. 'You mean to say my life should change once I become a Christian? Why is that?' People ask those kinds of questions now, because the link between identity and how you behave is weak.

The identity of a child of God

The end of Luke 10 actually addresses this crucial subject of true identity for the Christian in a very radical and wonderful way. The parable of the Good Samaritan has much to say to us. It has many old and true lessons about love and neighbourliness. But it is also very relevant to our contemporary situation. In particular, it unpacks to us what it is to have the identity of a true child of God. That is what these verses can be understood as teaching us.

We can look at it in three sections. First of all, let's look at verses 25 to 28, which are the introduction to the parable, where we have Jesus and the lawyer in conversation. We are introduced to this man – and he is a man with an identity: 'On one occasion an expert in the law stood up.' He is an expert in Old Testament Jewish law and the understanding the Jews had of it. That is his job and that is the way he sees himself: 'I am an expert.'

He asks Jesus: 'Teacher, what must I do to inherit eternal life?' So, who are the parties to the conversation here? We have Jesus and we have an expert in the Old Testament law: two Jewish people speaking together. Jewish people of the first century would have assumed that the true people of God would inherit God's kingdom, God's new age of eternal life. So when the lawyer asks: 'What must I do to inherit eternal life?', it is another way of asking: 'What does someone have to do to be part of the true people of God?' So we can legitimately re-jig the question to read: 'What does someone have to do to have the identity of belonging to God, of belonging to God's people?' That is what this expert is actually asking.

He is testing Jesus because Jesus is causing trouble to the Jewish establishment by his radical teaching. He wants to know whether Jesus is orthodox according to the Old Testament. Jesus' reply is absolutely orthodox, but with a sting in the tail for the expert. Jesus said: 'What is written in the law? How do you read it?'

The man answered: 'Love the Lord your God with all your heart, and with all your soul, and with all your strength, and with all your mind; and love your neighbour as yourself.'

'You have answered correctly,' Jesus replied. 'Do this and you will live.'

Walking with God, keeping his laws, his covenant, this is the mark of truly belonging to God's people. For an expert in the law, it is not merely knowing about these things but doing these things which mark people out as truly God's people.

We too must never fail to get hold of this, as Christians. Great Christians are not necessarily intellectuals, but they are doers. 'If anyone considers himself religious and yet does not keep a tight rein on his tongue, he deceives himself and his religion is worthless,' says James. 'Religion that God our Father accepts as pure and faultless is this: to look after orphans and widows in their distress and to keep oneself from being polluted by the world' (James 1:26,27). Don't fall into the trap, Jesus is telling us, of merely having expert knowledge. It is *doing* that marks people out.

Unlike our consumer society with its throw-away identities, Jesus underlines that true identity of people is not shown by their clothes, their race, their education or their gender, but by their behaviour. He is saying that there is a link between true identity and the way people behave, and you can tell the true people of God when they actually walk in God's ways. But our consumer society is seeking to undermine and reverse this link. So beware, Christian.

The second great commandment
With the exchange between Jesus and the expert in mind, we can see how the rest of the passage can be understood. The two great commands, to love God and to love our neighbour, had been mentioned as marks of God's true

people. So what is the rest of the passage? The parable of the Good Samaritan is Jesus' exposition of the second commandment to love our neighbour as ourselves. Jesus is saying that true identity is shown by the way people live, in particular by following the great commands to love God and to love our neighbours.

But in verse 29, 'The man wanted to justify himself, so he asked Jesus: "Who is my neighbour?" ' He wants to fence things off and set limits, so he asks: 'Who have I got to go out of my way to help?' In reply, Jesus told the story of the good Samaritan.

The fulcrum of the parable on which everything turns is this: the man lying half-dead in the road is unidentifiable. That is the crucial thing. There would be many groups, different races, different Jewish sects, different religious backgrounds, all kinds of different people in Palestine. They would have been distinguished by their clothes, by their accent or by something else. But here is a man that cannot be labelled, because he is unconscious and he is naked. He is only a human being in need. If one asks: 'Is he one of ours?', there is no way of knowing. As such he presents us with the litmus test. The man with no identity lying in the road becomes a test of the true identity of those people who walk up and down the road past him, as to whether or not they really are the people of God.

Beyond the image

With this in mind, the first thing which the parable does is to teach us to look beyond the outward image, which our consumer society is so keen on, to the heart. In verse 31, the priest comes down the road, perhaps in his flowing religious garments, the epitome of religion. Outwardly, he is definitely kosher. But, for whatever reason, he passes by on the other side, ignoring the man and ignoring God's covenant command to love his neighbour. Perhaps he is late for his religious service. Perhaps he does not want to get himself ceremonially unclean by touching someone who may be a Gentile. Perhaps he was worried that the robbers were still around waiting for someone to stop so that they could gain another victim. But for whatever reason, he passes by and shows that, for all his outward image, he does not belong to the people of God.

In verse 32, the Levite comes. He is a teacher, and perhaps he is carrying a copy of his Bible, a part of the Old Testament Scriptures. I am sure that it would be the very version that he would say was the most accurate. But as he comes to the man, he does not obey those Scriptures that he carries and that he teaches. He passes by. And for all his outward image, he shows no sign of belonging to the people of God.

Look past the outward image. People come in their sober suits and carrying their Bibles to the Reformed church. Others lift their hands in the Charismatic congregation in praise. There is nothing wrong with either of those things in themselves. But on their own, they mean nothing. Because only having an image you project is nothing. The true mark is a heart which loves God and other people, and is obedient to him, not perfectly – no-one is perfect this side of heaven – but which is genuinely seeking to be obedient and does really respond to God's commands.

At last, along that road comes a different man, a despised Samaritan. It is worthwhile just to underline the fact that there was religious and racial tension between the Jews and the Samaritans. Jesus himself had run into this problem just previously (Luke 9:52-53). He was on his way to Jerusalem and sent messengers on ahead of him into a Samaritan village to get things ready for him. But the people there did not welcome him because he was heading for Jerusalem. Jesus' disciples were very upset: 'Shall we call down fire from heaven and blast them off the face of the earth?' 'No, no,' says Jesus, 'that's not the way, let's go on somewhere else.'

But back to Jesus' story. Eventually, down the road comes a Samaritan, despised by the Jews. Again, the outward image is shattered. Do not assess people or deal with them in terms of caricatures. This man has every reason, humanly speaking, to pass by. The Jews and the Samaritans are enemies. But instead he went to the unidentifiable man, beaten up and unconscious. The Samaritan bandaged his wounds, pouring on oil and wine, then put the man on his own donkey and brought him to an inn and took care of him.

Here is a man who obeys the covenant law, even though racially the Jews would put him outside the covenant. There is in his heart a love, a mercy, that is not put off by possible dangers or the expense of a situation. There is in his heart a mercy which is not compromised by social or national prejudices. There is in his heart a mercy which is not limited by what other people might think of his actions. He has the mark of being in God's covenant.

The question mark

Expert in the law, you go and do the same things as this Samaritan. You are trying to limit your responsibility by asking: 'Who is my neighbour?' The very fact that you asked that question is a sign that, for all your expertise, you have never really known God. If you knew God, you would love people because they are made in the image of God. You would love them whoever they are, whatever their background, whatever their religion, because they are made in his image. The question mark is not over who you think your neighbour is, it is over you, expert in the law, unless your heart is changed and you follow in the footsteps of this Samaritan.

Let's make this a sharp lesson to us. The true test of our Christianity comes when there is a risk involved. It is easy to be a Christian when there is no risk. It is easy to be a Christian when whatever situation you face is right there in the Bible and you can just look up the answer and say: 'I'll just stick by the rules.' In a sense, that's only half a test of your spirituality. Anyone who does not take Scripture seriously is not listening to God. The test comes when the answer to the situation you face is not directly in the Bible, and it is a bit dangerous and a bit risky. When you are faced with that situation, what controls you then? Is it fear? Is it what others might think? Is it self-protection? Or is it the love of God? That's the litmus test. The Samaritan, who has all the wrong signals outwardly, inwardly has the right heart. It is not outward image that is required, but obedience from the heart.

One of the things I want to ask about this story is, why did Jesus choose a Samaritan? I can't say exactly, but one of the things that occurs to me is that a Samaritan in a Jewish society on that Jericho road was a blessedly despised man. He had nothing to lose and nothing to prove. He wasn't having to play to the gallery at all. Everybody looked down on him and so he was free to serve God. He was a broken man in that respect. Unless our experience of God has so humbled us that before the eyes of the world we have got nothing to prove and nothing to lose, unless our experience of God has broken us like that, then we will never serve God aright. Such an experience of true conversion breaks us, it makes us realise we really are sinners, and that only the grace of God can save us. Truly humbled, we are set free to get involved with people. The mark of the covenant comes upon us in that way.

The first commandment too

However, there is not just one commandment. There are two great commandments, and both are linked together and never detached from one another in the Scriptures. We are called to love the Lord as well as love our neighbour. Both are necessary, so Luke now puts in the story of Martha and Mary.

> As Jesus and his disciples were on their way, he came to a village where a woman named Martha opened her home to him. She had a sister called Mary, who sat at the Lord's feet listening to what he said. But Martha was distracted by all the preparations that had to be made (verses 38-40).

We should show love to our neighbours, not because they happen to be of our group or our race or whatever, but simply because they are human beings made in the image of God. But who is that God? Who is the Lord whose image

92

people were originally made as a pattern of? Who is God in whose image we are made?

He is Jesus. To love the Lord with all your heart, your soul, your strength, and your mind, is to sit at Jesus' feet. To sit at someone's feet is equivalent to studying under that person. Do you remember what it says of the apostle Paul in the Book of Acts (22:3, AV), that he was brought up at the feet of Gamaliel? He learned from that great religious teacher. Mary sits learning at the feet of Jesus. She gets her theology from him.

But to sit at someone's feet is also to put yourself at his disposal. Remember again, how in the Book of Acts some believers sold their fields and they laid the money at *the apostles' feet*, saying: 'You do with it what you want to, for the good of the church and for the good of God's kingdom' (Acts 4:32-37). Mary, at the feet of Jesus, is saying, 'I am at your disposal, learning from you.' She is a true disciple of Jesus.

Martha's busyness guarantees nothing. Sadly, often, busyness can be just another image that we want to project to impress people: 'Oh, how busy they are for the Lord!' Don't mistake my meaning; there is nothing wrong with busyness. But if our motive is merely to impress others, we are in trouble.

The consumer society, like Martha, is a distracted society, a cluttered society. 'You must try this option. Haven't you done that? Haven't you been there? Have you seen this?' There are so many things to do, and there is no time to sit at the feet of Jesus.

The consumer society is also a critical society. Martha comes and says: 'Lord, don't you care that my sister is not

93

helping me?' The consumer society is a judgmental society, it has been trained to see the faults in all the goods and to get the better deal, and if there are faults in other people, we can soon sniff those out as well.

'No,' says Jesus, 'away with all that.' Real life is not about having this and that and the other and getting involved in absolutely every possible choice. Real life is about one thing, about sitting, first of all, at Jesus' feet and him being first in your life. Even before we serve him, we must come and sit at his feet and learn from him. That is the mark of truly belonging to the people of God. Our true love for God is seen by our time spent with Jesus.

What are we to do if, looking at ourselves, we see the marks of truly belonging to God's people are not really there? What if our hearts are caught up in the consumer mindset and are not right with God? What if we see we have more of an image which we want to project, a mask, rather than a true identity of belonging to God? What if we are more like the expert in the law, and the priest, and the Levite? What are we to do?

We are to come and sit at the feet of Jesus and receive from him. Come not first to serve him, but to let Jesus serve us. He came as a servant to give his life as a ransom for our sins, that we might be forgiven. He knows all about the many times that we have passed by, all the many times we have sinned and not done as we ought to have done. Come and sit at his feet, and weep out your sins, and receive forgiveness from him. He came to make it possible for us to be changed, not just on the outward image level, but in the heart. He will give us the Holy Spirit who will write the law of God on our hearts. Then there will be such affection for the Lord that, though we may still struggle and fail to obey God perfectly, we will obey him truly.

Many people in our society, as I said, are lost; they don't know who they are. We will only find our true identity at the feet of Jesus. There, we will discover that we were made *by* God and made *for* God. Like everyone else, we have rebelled against God and are deserving of destruction and we need his grace and his forgiveness. Yet as we come to Christ and receive these things, who do we become? We become the true children of God, marked within by his Spirit, forgiven through the blood by Christ, singled out as his with a new heart within us. Jesus, therefore, is saying, 'Throw away the shop-around identities and images of the consumer society, because they can never satisfy you. They will leave you lost in a sea of not knowing who you really are. Come to me, find your true identity in me. You are called to a lifestyle not rooted in the shifting sands of this world, but in God, in the eternal permanence and stability of the Lord.'

CHAPTER 6

FREEDOM AND CUSTOMER SERVICE

Please read: Galatians 5:16-25

---

[16]So I say, live by the Spirit, and you will not gratify the desires of the sinful nature. [17]For the sinful nature desires what is contrary to the Spirit, and the Spirit what is contrary to the sinful nature. They are in conflict with each other, so that you do not do what you want. [18]But if you are led by the Spirit, you are not under law.

[19]The acts of the sinful nature are obvious: sexual immorality, impurity and debauchery; [20]idolatry and witchcraft; hatred, discord, jealousy, fits of rage, selfish ambition, dissensions, factions [21]and envy; drunkenness, orgies, and the like. I warn you, as I did before, that those who live like this will not inherit the kingdom of God.

[22]But the fruit of the Spirit is love, joy, peace, patience, kindness, goodness, faithfulness, [23]gentleness and self-control. Against such things there is no law. [24]Those who belong to Christ Jesus have crucified the sinful nature with its passions and desires. [25]Since we live by the Spirit, let us keep in step with the Spirit.

All the cleverest heresies are half true. They often address vital issues, but from a position which is only a little off centre. That is why they are so persuasive and attractive.

Galatians 5 is a chapter concerned with moral freedom

for the Christian. In verse 1, Paul says: 'It is for freedom, that Christ has set us free'; and he further says in verse 13: 'You, my brothers, were called to be free.' We Christians have been released from the condemnation of the law of God against us. We have been set at liberty, released from the bondage of sin. In Christ we are free from the fear of death. We are a people who are emancipated in Christ, not enslaved or coerced, but at liberty under God to opt for what we think is best in Christ. In this liberty, with Christian wisdom, we can therefore creatively express ourselves. We are all given different talents by God, and it is our responsibility to use them in the most worthwhile way for the glory of God and the good of the world. We each have something unique to contribute to the kingdom of God as we freely serve the Lord.

Both consumerism and Christianity value the idea of liberty, and freedom of choice. Consumerism takes you to the shop and says: 'You choose! It's up to you – express yourself.' Personal choice makes people feel significant. It is a way of making a statement about oneself. The things I choose to buy express who I am, or the image I wish to present to others.

Christianity also sees the value of individual freedom. Christianity sees people as uniquely made in the image of God, with a creative ability to choose different courses of action. This makes us significant beings. As the image of God, under his authority, we too are to be little creators. We are given the so-called cultural mandate of Genesis 1:28,29 to subdue and nurture the earth and bring it to its fruition. Hence we have all the arts, sciences and technologies. As Christians we are given the gospel command to go into all the world and preach Christ to all (Matt. 28:19,20). While staying true to God and his message, we are to use our God-given minds, and prayerfully think creatively about how to bring the gospel to our generation.

A matter of choice

As I said, all the most subtle heresies have a lot of truth in them, and this emphasis on freedom of the individual is the Christian truth which the heresy of consumerism has latched on to in particular. Freedom of choice is a marvellous gift. But it raises important questions at the practical level, let alone the theological level.

We can make our choices. But choice according to which criteria? How do we define what is 'best' when it comes to making the best choice? And who is this individual, this self which is to do the choosing?

When we ask questions like that, then although on the surface Christianity and consumerism have this matter of freedom in common, they come into very fundamental conflict with one another. For example, Paul declares in Galatians 5:13-15 that true freedom is not about self-indulgence, but about service: 'You, my brothers, were called to be free. But do not use your freedom to indulge the sinful nature; rather, serve one another in love. The entire law is summed up in a single command: "Love your neighbour as yourself." If you keep on biting and devouring each other, watch out or you will be destroyed by each other.' Self-indulgence is not true freedom, but service is. No doubt Paul also has in mind the service of God, but in particular he mentions here service to other people.

So, with our concern to investigate how to live as

Christian disciples in a consumer society, we are going to look at this passage and think a little about the matter of individual freedom in the light of what Paul wrote.

Inner conflict

In verses 16 to 18 Paul writes of the inner conflict that goes on within Christians. Behind the alternatives of self-indulgence or service is the battle between the sinful nature and the Spirit. The sinful nature is our fallen nature and it is inherently selfish and bound up with this world. It is the nature into which we are naturally born. But the Spirit is the indwelling Holy Spirit who has created a new self in us. The mark of the new birth, of truly being a Christian, is that the Holy Spirit has wrought this great change in us. We are not perfect, but we have been changed and now have a genuine love for Christ and the things of God, his Word and his people.

Therefore, within the Christian there is the old self, which belongs to the past and to this world, and there is the new self which has been newly created in Christ Jesus. This creates the internal tension which we never entirely escape until we reach heaven. Verse 17 highlights this: 'For the sinful nature desires what is contrary to the Spirit, and the Spirit what is contrary to the sinful nature. They are in conflict with each other, so that you do not do what you want.'

Some people when they become Christians cannot understand why they still have problems. They cannot understand why they are not perfect immediately, and so are thrown into tremendous depression every time they make a mistake, or fall into sin. Pastors often have to speak to sincere Christians on this subject. Many faithful people, as they go on in the Christian life, feel that they are worse sinners than when they were first saved. Actually what is happening to them is that, as the Holy Spirit continues to transform and renovate their lives, their consciences are becoming more sensitive to spiritual and moral issues. As they grow in Christ, the light of his holiness dawns more clearly upon their souls and more of their blemishes are shown up. To such people, John writes: 'If we say we have no sin we deceive ourselves.... but if we confess our sins he is faithful and just and will forgive us' (1 John 1:8,9). It was the Lord Jesus who taught his *disciples* to pray 'Forgive us our trespasses'. It comes as such a relief to many Christians to realize that though we are new creatures in Christ we will not be perfect until we get to heaven.

It is worth recognising that the ethos of consumerism is directed to feeding our old self, to feeding the flesh. Consumerism is all about this world, not the things of God, and therefore it develops and massages that 'me first' perspective. The things of this world are made attractive to sinners – and consumerism feeds the sinful nature. As Christians we need to recognise the reality of this, especially as we live in a culture that is particularly geared to this outlook.

The rise of advertising
Studying around this subject of the consumer culture led me to read about the industrialization of America. The United States is the leading nation of the Western world, so its history has relevance to us all. Until the twentieth century, most American homes were sites not only of

consumption but of production. People made things at home. As late as 1850, six out of ten people in the USA worked on farms. They made their own tools, their own furniture, grew crops, looked after animals, they were self-reliant. Then along came the industrial revolution, and everything changed very quickly.

As the factory system and mass production came to dominance, it displaced home production. Factories took over. People began moving from the land into the cities. The economic system of the factory could produce many more goods than the existing population in America, with its habits of self-reliance and frugality, actually wanted or needed or could afford to consume. Let me give an example. James Buchanan-Duke was a cigarette manufacturer. He bought two cigarette-making machines and went into production. He found that almost immediately he could produce 240,000 cigarettes a day, which was more than the entire USA market smoked in one day. The point I am making is that such over-production became the rule, not the exception, throughout the economy, not just in cigarettes, but in all kinds of things.

Here with the advent of industrialization there emerged this huge gap between production and consumption. The obvious question that arose was how that gap was to be closed. Simply speaking, two options were available. Either cut down production and with that the possible profits, or teach people to consume more than they actually needed. It is not surprising that it was the second of these options which was pursued.

Manufacturers decided to seek to increase our consumption. People had to be taught to move away from habits of thrift and traditional home-skills and to take on an attitude of ready spending and reliance on manufacturers. This is a great key to understanding the mass psychology of our society. The whole marketing and advertising industries thus came into being.

Against contentment

An interesting article in an old edition of *Christianity Today* quotes from what was called the Thompson Red Book on Advertising from 1901. In this there is a little sentence which describes advertising at the turn of the century: 'Advertising aims to teach people that they have wants which they did not recognise before, and where such wants can be supplied.'[1] Advertising was to set out to make people 'realize' that they have wants and needs that must be fulfilled, even though they were unaware of them before!

In effect, this is a cultivation of dissatisfaction. Even in the best of circumstances the sinful hearts of fallen men and women will always know an emptiness, for we were made for God and are now cut off from him. We were made for the Spirit, and the flesh can never satisfy. Instead of contentment we are prone to feel that things could be better. That is what is being played on in advertising. The twentieth century in the western world has been largely taken over by that massaging of dissatisfaction. Advertising frequently has that end in view – to make us discontent with what we already have and encourage us to get more. We live in a culture specifically geared to speaking to the sinful nature.

---

1. Rodney Clapp, 'Why the devil takes VISA', *Christianity Today*.

Self-worship

Another element closely allied to the age of advertising and consumption is the ethos of self-worship, the psychology of self which is assumed as healthy in our times.

Hand-in-hand with the growth of industrial society has come the rise of popular psychology which says that happiness and true fulfilment in life is about self-actualisation, self-esteem, self-assertiveness, self-knowledge. The 'me generation' is the name it is frequently given. 'You must do what feels good for you.' That is what the agony aunts and many psychologists will advise (though one must not brand all psychologists with this idea).

Paul Vitz has written a book which has become a modern classic among thinking Christians. It is called *Psychology as Religion: The Cult of Self-Worship*. In it, he says this:

> It has certainly proved convenient that just as Western economies began to need consumers, there developed an ideology hostile to discipline, to obedience, and to delaying of gratification. Self-ism's clear advocacy of experience now and its rejection of inhibition or repression was a boon to the advertising industry, which was finding that the returns on appeals to social status and product quality were diminishing. Most of the short expressions and catchwords of self-theory make excellent advertising copy: Do it now! Have a new experience! Honour thyself.[2]

We need to be aware that this is the world in which we are living. As we seek to be free, as we are engaged in this conflict between the sinful nature and the Spirit, we need to realise we are caught up in this general malaise of consumerism which will drag us one way and one way only.

---

2. Paul Vitz, *Psychology as Religion: The Cult of Self-Worship*, Paternoster, 1994.

Isn't it so sad when even Christianity comes to us in a consumer package? Even religion is marketed to us. Some large Christian conferences are geared to a consumer mentality: there are choices of seminars, and topics, and different styles of worship to suit each kind of religious culture. Then there is the exhibition and selling area. It is set out like a great shopping mall. All the books of the main speakers are pressed on us from the platform. All the conference addresses and worship songs are instantly available on audio tape. They are almost marketed in a way which is within a hair's breadth of intimating that one can buy spirituality when one buys these things. Then again, only certain Christian companies are allowed to advertise in certain ways to protect the market share of this bookseller or that music publisher. It has become big business. All this seems so different from the spirit of evangelical conferences from years gone by, when the great emphasis was to make the convention a time of fellowship and meeting with God.

Obviously I am not against Christian books or Christian tapes, but the whole thing seems to be so commercially driven that one wonders what the Lord really thinks of it all. Yes, there had to be a place where people could buy their sacrifices, and whatever else was necessary for the worship of God, but did they really have to turn the temple of God into a market place rather than a house of prayer?

Two philosophies

There is the inner conflict in every Christian between the flesh and the Spirit. The environment in which we now live in the Western world is acutely tuned to the 'needs' of the flesh.

In verses 19 to 23, Paul now goes into a deeper description of the contrasting protagonists of the flesh and the Spirit. In case we fall into the error of thinking that anything that feels good must be of the Holy Spirit (and many people do fall into that way of thinking), Paul spells out for us the telltale marks of the two protagonists.

How do you really know what is of the flesh and what is of the Spirit? Well, says Paul in verses 19-21: 'The acts of the sinful nature are obvious: sexual immorality, impurity and debauchery; idolatry and witchcraft...' – these things may even be dressed up in a cloak of religion, but if that is the direction they are going in, you know what is the real root of them – 'hatred, discord, jealousy, fits of rage, selfish ambition, dissensions, factions and envy; drunkenness, orgies, and the like. I warn you, as I did before, that those who live like this will not inherit the kingdom of God.' If that is someone's predominant behaviour and attitude, then God has never really come into his life, whatever he may say. The Spirit is not in people if he is never actually producing the right kind of life in them. Though they may be religious, they are lost.

But, by contrast to the acts of the sinful nature, 'the fruit of the Spirit is love, joy, peace (especially love for God and joy in God and peace in God), patience, kindness, goodness, faithfulness, gentleness and self-control. Against such things there is no law.' There is no law, no condemnation against such a way of life. Can you see the marks? Can you identify the protagonists? Again, in the context of the consumer culture in which we live, it is worth pointing out a couple of things.

First, there is the contrast between two different

philosophies of life. For the sinful nature, life is all about action and experience. It is oriented in that way, it is about outwardly doing things or having things come to you. The idea is that the self, what you are, is fine. All it needs is to express itself or to have new experiences, new activities, new things added to it. The self is great. That is what much modern psychology says, isn't it? Basically we are good, it is only that we need some more things added to us or else we need to handle some things a little differently. Of course, that is also precisely the philosophy of consumerism. There is nothing wrong with you that a bit of shopping, a new suit, a new holiday, a new car, will not sort out. And you'll feel great. There is nothing wrong with you that a new therapy or technique of going about things will not solve. Do you need to feel happy? Go and buy something. Indulge in a little retail therapy, you will feel better with something new. That's the philosophy of the sinful nature.

But the philosophy of the Spirit is very different. What the Spirit is telling us is that life is about inner attitudes and it is the self that needs to change. The self is not all right as it is. It is corrupt at root and rebellious against God. It needs to be born again. It does not need a touching up with a few elegant acquisitions, rather it requires total transformation. It needs to be broken and reconstructed by the radical cleansing power of the Holy Spirit. The self needs to have new Spirit-produced characteristics to come to fruition in it. It needs love and joy and peace, things from within, patience and kindness and goodness towards other people, self-control with respect to oneself.

We could also contrast the way of the flesh and the way

of the Spirit in the area of timescale. Paul speaks about the *acts* of the sinful nature. Normally we think of an act as something instantaneous. We do it. It is a matter of 'now'. Someone may nurture hatred for a long time, but that is only because the appropriate moment to vent his revenge has not been afforded. If he could he would express all that hatred in an instant. The consumer attitude dovetails with the instantaneous world of gratification which is so much a part of the flesh. We want it now. For example, when Lloyd's launched Access cards in 1972, the advertising slogan read, 'Access takes the waiting out of wanting.' With credit cards you can have it now and pay later.

By contrast the way of the Spirit is spoken of in terms of *fruit*. The timescale of the Spirit is different. No one ever saw a tree produce fruit in an instant. Fruit takes time to grow. If gardeners try to force growth too quickly, the fruit is lost. There is a control and a more gentle pace. The way of the Spirit includes 'self-control', and the ability to postpone immediate gratification in order to pursue a greater good.

The two ways are very different.

Two different outcomes

Secondly, there is a contrast flagged up here for us by Paul when he says that the outcomes of those two different ways of life are very different. Paul says concerning those who live according to the way of the sinful nature: 'I warn you, as I did before, that those who live like this will not inherit the kingdom of God' (verse 21). Such a way of life does not lead to heaven, it leads to hell.

I have to say that is not only true in the life to come, but it is true, in a sense, in this life too. Reflect for a moment on the area of sex. There are all kinds of books about the 'joy of sex' on the shelves of the major secular bookshops. All these 'self-help' books are based on this self-orientated, self-preoccupied, consumer psychology. These are being sold with the implication that a relationship or a marriage will really take off if this or that technique is put into practice. Yet, despite the sale of millions of copies of these guidebooks of so-called sexual satisfaction, what do we actually see in our world? Divorce is at an unprecedented level. Women are demeaned in the most pathetic ways. Outside of marriage, the average length of a cohabiting relationship is twenty-nine months.

These things are not bringing true satisfaction. They do not help because they are not addressing the real problem. The real problem is the selfishness that is within, and people want to use marriage and sex within marriage in a selfish way, focusing on getting satisfaction, finding 'joy' for the sinful self rather than in a way that is loving, serving and helpful to the partner. Thus it is in the Western world. According to very good evidence, a third of children involved in divorce never recover psychologically. Where does the way of the flesh lead? It leads to destruction.

Are you caught up in that? Are you trapped in worldly ways of organising your life and thinking? Trapped in the world's idea of what a relationship with someone should be, what your partner in life should be like, rather than what the Scriptures say you should be looking for in a wife or a husband? If you are, you will not give yourself in true commitment to Christ because you are actually trapped in the world's outlook.

Perhaps this same worldly attitude pervades your working life as well. Are you trapped in the world's view of ambition and getting on in life? Are you running yourself into the ground, destroying yourself in a job which makes ever more demands upon you, rather than saying: 'It doesn't matter if I don't reach the top. What matters is knowing God and walking with him.'

The pursuit of self brings devastation. It does so because we were never made to be centred on ourselves, but centred on God.

By contrast, the fruit of the Spirit brings life. When we walk in God's law we walk according to the Maker's instructions. Those instructions are for our good. They will do us no harm. Against such things as Christian love and joy, gentleness, self-control, there is no law. Those things bring no condemnation. They bring no destruction.

In Christ and his ways there is true freedom. God says, 'Go for it. There is a great wide area marked out by my commands and you can use all your creative ability to serve me there.' That is life! Here we can express our new self. Here we are free to find expression for all the beautiful things which God has put within us by his Holy Spirit. The latent potential of what we can be in God can flourish to our benefit and God's glory.

So the two contrasting protagonists are explained to us. They are different philosophies of life, they have different ends and this battle is going on within.

Freedom in the Spirit

The question now comes: how can we seek to ensure that the desires of the Spirit predominate over the desires of the sinful nature, so that we walk in true freedom and inherit eternal life? Paul replies, it depends on the attitudes that we adopt to the two protagonists, to the sinful nature and to the Spirit. He mentions two aspects.

First, there is a required crucifixion: 'Those who belong to Christ Jesus have crucified the sinful nature with its passions and desires' (verse 24). The old self needs to be crucified. There is a part of us that needs to be put to death. Because it belongs to the old life, it is shot through with sin, and therefore needs to be nailed up and crucified. Having come to Christ, we have crucified the flesh, that is, we have admitted that sinful self and the things of this world are spiritually bankrupt, horrifically offensive to God, and only lead to destruction. Says Paul, 'If that is what you have done, live in a way that is congruent with it. So take up your cross daily, deny yourself and follow Jesus in the practical matters of life.'

Be a man or woman who thinks differently from the brainwashed consumers around you. Fight that desire to keep spending in order to have some new acquisition. Do not be taken in by the 'gospel' of consumerism which promises happiness through money and things. Remember the words of Christ, 'What will it profit a man if he gains the whole world but loses his soul?' Remember the words of Jesus, 'It is more blessed to give than to receive.' Deny the cravings of the old self. Put them to death. Fight the desire to have everything immediately. Learn the patience which is such a hallmark of the Spirit.

If you are married, be a husband who sacrifices himself for the good of his family and for the good of his wife. Be a man who is not a lord over the family for everyone else to run around, but who is a servant leader who loves his family by denying himself to give to them. It is not just a matter of money, but it includes things like time and interest and effort. If you are a wife, know that material things will not make a happy family. Often large houses, where every child has its own room and own TV and computer, are inhabited by families which live apart under the same roof. They may come together for meals, and then they once again disappear into their own little 'haven' which no one else is allowed to enter, and there they learn to live in selfish isolation.

When all the world is living for material things it is difficult, it is hard, to go against the tide. A self-crucifixion is required.

Let me quote from John Stott:

> Crucifixion was a horrible, brutal form of execution, yet it illustrates graphically what our attitude to our fallen nature is to be. We are not to coddle and cuddle it, not to pamper or spoil it, not to give it any encouragement or even toleration, instead we are to be ruthlessly fierce in rejecting it.[3]

Note those words 'ruthlessly' and 'rejecting'. To take that darling sin, which will nuzzle up to the old self, and make itself look as amiable and as cute as possible, and nail it up until it dies, takes grit and courage. The devil will come and tell you that you are a fool. He will tell you that there is no need for such 'fanaticism'. But Paul is elaborating the teaching of Jesus about taking up the cross and following him, he is telling us what happens when we reach the place of execution, where the actual crucifixion takes place.

---

3. John Stott, *Galatians*, The Bible Speaks Today, IVP.

Luther writes that 'Christian people nail their flesh to the cross, so that although the flesh be yet alive, yet it cannot perform that which it would do, forasmuch as it is bound both hand and foot and fast-nailed to the cross.'[4] And, warns John Stott: 'If we are not ready to crucify ourselves in this decisive manner we shall soon find that, instead, we are crucifying the Son of God all over again. The essence of apostasy is changing sides from that of the crucified to that of the crucifier.'[5] That is true. If we don't crucify those sins in our lives, they do begin to grow up, they do begin to strangle spiritual life within, it does lead so sadly away from Jesus.

Many church elders know how sins take over people in the church and those who once said that they did love Christ have walked out on him. How many have set out with perhaps a little business in the town and their shop has begun to do well. Next they are working all hours and are missing from mid-week home groups or the prayer meeting. Not long after that, they have enough money to buy a 'holiday home' and spend many weekends away from Sunday worship. They drift away from the fellowship. Next they are making excuses that they must open their shop on a Sunday to stay in trade, because competitors are doing so. It is the parable of the sower all over again. The thorns and weeds of the cares of this world and the love of money are strangling their spiritual life away.

The whole attitude of 'self first' is a deadly trap. Don't cuddle the old self, crucify it. It is a painful thing, but it is like cutting out the cancer which is only going to destroy

---

4. Martin Luther, quoted by John Stott, ibid.
5. John Stott, ibid.

you. Remember that when we feel we are being sucked in. It is painful to put it to death, to turn away from it, but remember you are cutting out the cancer. The required crucifixion is so necessary in our society today.

The new self

But that is not the end, thank goodness. Though the old self is to be crucified, the new self is to be encouraged and affirmed.

The things of the Spirit in us are to be built up and nurtured within us. 'Since we live by the Spirit, let us keep in step with the Spirit' (verse 25). We are not to be tripping up the Spirit as it were. We are not to be getting in the Spirit's way in our lives. Rather we are to be in step with him, walking with him, so that our new selves that God loves and values so much may blossom and grow. God gave his Son for us. You are so valuable. Those new selves are cherished by God. We are his beloved children. He wants to see us grow to maturity in the Spirit, not damage and disfigure ourselves in the world.

What is it to keep in step with the Spirit? Let me give some ideas. *It is to put God first every day.* Who is to be the centre of worship in your life? The Lord is. You find your true place when you put the Lord first in your life in practical matters, seeking him each day, letting him guide your ambitions etc. God first, instead of self.

It is to be led by faith, rather than by sight. The consumer society says: 'Look at this, look at this, look at this!' It is all about using your eyes and your physical senses. The Scripture says, no, it is not sight that will lead you to the truth, it is faith. It is understanding the Scriptures, it is believing on the Lord Jesus Christ, it is walking in his way, walking by faith as Abraham did, as Moses did, as Paul did. Faith sees the things which are invisible. What is seen is passing away, but what is unseen is eternal.

It is service instead of self-indulgence. Keeping in step with the Spirit is looking upon other people and seeing what we can do to encourage them and build them up, instead of putting our own sinful selves at the centre of things. That means in a way, focusing on community instead of individualism. Our consumer society is such an individualistic society. We shall think about this in the next chapter. Don't get me wrong, there is a proper individualism, for God does love the individual. But he calls us into community. We don't need to pry into everybody's affairs, but he does call us to love one another. The consumer society is saying: 'Stay at home, shut the door, watch the television, and get your own bits and pieces together, just be yourself on your own.' That is not what God wants. God is calling a people out from the world which pushes us towards isolation, into a togetherness before him as his people of worship. We are to be oriented towards community, in our neighbourhoods, in the church, in the family, rather than the individualism of our society. Keep in step with the Spirit. The Spirit is seeking to build the church together. Are you in step with him?

What does it mean to keep in step with the Spirit? The secular society is a prayerless society. It does not believe in a God who sovereignly rules the world and answers his children's requests. It relies on its own abilities, and, knowing their limitations, often worries. According to some psychotherapists, the occurrence of depression in the West has increased ten-fold since 1945. We need to be different. We need *prayer instead of anxiety*. Instead of looking to yourself and panicking saying: 'What can I do, there is this great trouble coming?', it means to go to the Lord and say: 'Father, I thank you that you are there. You are my God, and I am bringing these things to you.' That is keeping in step with the Spirit.

Keeping in step with the Spirit is *being oriented towards changing inwardly*. Inwardly changing to become more like the Lord Jesus Christ.

This is true freedom, because when the things of this world are not used in God's way, they begin to take over, they begin to enslave us, they begin to bring us into addiction rather than freedom. The story is told of an old man who lived in the mountains somewhere. He had two dogs and the whole neighbourhood knew that the dogs fought one another all the time. Someone said to the man: 'I hear your dogs do a lot of fighting with each other. Which one of them wins in these fights?' The old man was quiet for a long time, and then he said with a smile: 'The one that wins is the one I feeds the most.'

Within us, there are two dogs – the self and the Spirit. Which one is going to win? 'The one I feeds the most.' Starve the sinful nature and feed the things of the Spirit, says Paul. 'Those who belong to Christ Jesus have crucified the sinful nature with its passions and desires. Since we live by the Spirit, let us keep in step with the Spirit.'

CHAPTER 7

THE CURRENCY OF COMMITMENT

Please read Luke 9:18-27; 57-62

¹⁸Once when Jesus was praying in private and his disciples were with him, he asked them, 'Who do the crowds say I am?'

¹⁹They replied, 'Some say John the Baptist; others say Elijah; and still others, that one of the prophets of long ago has come back to life.'

²⁰'But what about you?' he asked. 'Who do you say I am?'

Peter answered, 'The Christ of God.'

²¹Jesus strictly warned them not to tell this to anyone. ²²And he said, 'The Son of Man must suffer many things and be rejected by the elders, chief priests and teachers of the law, and he must be killed and on the third day be raised to life.'

²³Then he said to them all: 'If anyone would come after me, he must deny himself and take up his cross daily and follow me. ²⁴For whoever wants to save his life will lose it, but whoever loses his life for me will save it. ²⁵What good is it for a man to gain the whole world, and yet lose or forfeit his very self? ²⁶If anyone is ashamed of me and my words, the Son of Man will be ashamed of him when he comes in his glory and in the glory of the Father and of the holy angels. ²⁷I tell you the truth, some who are standing here will not taste death before they see the kingdom of God' (18-27).

[57]As they were walking along the road, a man said to him, 'I will follow you wherever you go.'

[58]Jesus replied, 'Foxes have holes and birds of the air have nests, but the Son of Man has no place to lay his head.'

[59]He said to another man, 'Follow me.'

But the man replied, 'Lord, first let me go and bury my father.'

[60]Jesus said to him, 'Let the dead bury their own dead, but you go and proclaim the kingdom of God.'

[61]Still another said, 'I will follow you, Lord; but first let me go back and say good-bye to my family.'

[62]Jesus replied, 'No one who puts his hand to the plough and looks back is fit for service in the kingdom of God' (57-62).

Have you ever sat down and asked: 'What do I want from my life?' I think most Christians probably hold fairly similar ambitions. We long for our lives to count. Here is a list of four areas in which we would probably like to make achievements.

Firstly, we want to accomplish something significant for the benefit of others and for Christ's kingdom. We want to serve God. Secondly, we earnestly desire to be loved and to love others, and therefore we thirst for deep relationships of various kinds. We want to go through our lives building friendships and fellowship. Thirdly, we want to grow in God and discover more of him. We want to 'know him' whom to know is life eternal. We want to experience more of his security and stability and joy in our lives and indeed to become more like his Son, the Lord

Jesus. And fourthly, we want to die well, we want to leave a good example.

Romantic ideas of commitment

They are worthy ambitions, yet not one of those ambitions can be attained in an instant. None of them can be realised without patience, perseverance, dedication and, often, sacrifice. In short, not one of them can be attained without commitment.

Commitment is vital. These passages from Luke's Gospel confront us with the idea of commitment. Verse 51 challenges us with the commitment of Jesus going to Jerusalem, there to be crucified, there to be raised from the dead and ascend into heaven. He was to enter glory through dreadful injustice and suffering, especially at the cross, for our salvation. 'As the time approached for him to be taken up to heaven, Jesus resolutely (with commitment) set out for Jerusalem.' Jesus' life was marked by courage, loyalty and commitment.

But the passage also confronts us with the commitment Christ requires of his disciples: 'No-one who puts his hand to the plough and looks back is fit for service in the kingdom of God' (verse 62). Probably most of us have a romantic image of commitment. We think highly of those who are committed to a noble cause. We can see, too, the benefits of commitment. Perhaps a few years ago we saw Linford Christie win his eighth European Championship in the 100 metres. He was thirty-seven years old and still winning. He only achieved that through commitment to his training. We admire him. So we acknowledge the benefits of commitment.

But a romantic image of commitment frequently dominates people. We applaud the benefits of commitment, but we dislike its demands. We shy away from it in practice because commitment always involves giving up certain freedoms and always involves taking on new obligations.

We are considering the question of living as disciples of Christ in a consumer society. We have defined consumerism loosely as that promise of happiness through material goods and services, pursued in a way which emphasises our own personal preferences and choices. There is such a vast array of goods and services on offer and our society is saying: 'You choose whatever you like, you express yourself; there are thousands of options for you to choose from.'

Keeping options open

It is inevitably a disparate society. Different people have different tastes. There is no uniformity. There is no reason to be nailed down to one thing. There is always something new to be doing and if what you are doing now eventually palls and gets on your nerves, you can choose something different.

In a society where people idolise choice, then keeping one's options open as much as possible becomes the order of the day. Commitment to one cause or course of action therefore becomes a currency which is of diminishing value in most people's eyes. We can observe this in almost every area of contemporary life.

We are a mobile society, we move from town to town; civic roots have virtually been destroyed.

We are the secular society, we don't want to be

committed to religion; 'it is a straitjacket,' people say.

We are the 'hire and fire' society; employers are rarely loyal to their employees when financial pressure is on. The idea of staying in one job for life seems to be an idea from a previous world, now lost forever. This is an overstatement, but these days it seems that employees are a disposable commodity. 'Work them until they burn out, then employ someone younger and do the same to them,' seems to be the philosophy among some managers.

We are the divorce society; we don't want to be committed to one partner, or committed to marriage. We want to be unfettered, able to move from one partner to another.

Sadly, even within the Christian world, commitment to church is sliding. One recent survey in the USA showed that the average length of stay in a local church is four years. Churches are, unfortunately, not families of people who walk the road together all the way to heaven. Instead churches are often a spiritual supermarket into which people come, take what they want, and go.

The only thing we are committed to is ourselves, and our pleasure. Talking to church leaders, to pastors, one finds that the great thing on their minds is commitment to Christ and to church life. 'Where has it gone?' they ask. The consumer society undermines all commitment, and commitment to the church is just one of the casualties.

This is a vast subject, but we are going to touch on it briefly, just under three major headings. We will use this passage in Luke 9 to focus our thoughts. We are going to see first of all the call to commitment; secondly, the fear of commitment; and thirdly, the rewards of commitment.

The call to commitment

The whole section of verses 57 to 62 revolves around the words, 'Follow me.' Ours is a generation which needs to be reminded that Christ's call to commitment is absolute. It is not partial, it is total. This passage brings that out. Jesus requires absolute commitment to himself. The mere words, 'Yes, Lord, I'll follow', are not enough. Thorough commitment is called for. These verses focus on the cost of discipleship and consist of three little dialogues woven around the word 'follow'. In verse 57 we read: 'I will follow you wherever you go.' In verse 59: 'Follow me,' says Jesus. In verse 61 another man says: 'I will follow you, Lord.'

What is it to follow Christ? Each of these three short exchanges underlines Christ's demands. Look at verses 57 and 58: 'As they were walking along the road, a man said to him, "I will follow you wherever you go." Jesus replied, "Foxes have holes and birds of the air have nests, but the Son of man has no place to lay his head." ' Jesus responds to the man's willing expression to follow him by saying, 'Hold on, do you realise what you are saying?' If you look back at verses 51 to 56, you will see that Jesus has just been refused hospitality by a Samaritan village. 'This is the kind of thing that happens to my followers,' Jesus intimates. 'Foxes have holes, birds of the air have nests, I don't have anywhere to lay my head tonight.'

There can be physical privation in the cause of following Christ. In this case, it is homelessness. We can think of Christians in our own day, living in lands unsympathetic to the Christian faith, who have had their villages attacked or their homes bulldozed. Jesus is saying, 'My call to commitment overrides even our natural desires for comfort and security. There is nothing wrong with security and comfort, but my call for commitment supersedes even those in someone's life. Do you really want to follow me?'

Secondly, in verses 59 to 60: 'He said to another man, "Follow me."' This is the other way around now. This is not someone offering to come, rather this is Jesus saying: 'I want you, follow me!' 'But the man replied, "Lord, first let me go and bury my father." Jesus said to him, "Let the dead bury their own dead, [Those who are spiritually out of contact with God, they are dead to God], but you go and proclaim the kingdom of God." ' In Luke 10 Jesus had sent out seventy-two disciples to proclaim the kingdom. Similarly, Jesus here takes the initiative in calling someone to such work. The man says: 'But please let me bury my father.' Burial of the dead was a religious duty among the Jews, taking precedence over all others. Priests who were not usually allowed to touch dead bodies could do so in the case of close relatives. So burial of a father to a Jew was a primary duty to family and society. But Jesus, astonishingly, says, 'My call to you overrides even that. My call to you is such that, if necessary, you are to put aside even natural obligations, put aside what people might think about you, and follow me.' His claim is absolute.

Then thirdly, in verse 61 and 62: 'Still another said, "I will follow you, Lord, but first let me go back and say good-bye to my family." Jesus replied: "No-one who puts his hand to the plough and looks back is fit for service in the kingdom of God." ' Obviously Jesus does not want us to neglect our families, but what he is saying is that in the end his commands to us must take precedence even over our natural affection and duties to our earthly families. He says, 'Only those who can plough a straight furrow, moving toward a mark without looking one way or the other, or being distracted for a moment even by legitimate family affections, can give the kind of single-mindedness that I require for service in my kingdom.'

These three dialogues then are dealing with the cost of discipleship that comes from attachment to Christ. Single-minded devotion to Jesus is required. Complete dedication is required. Now that is astonishing for our world, but that is what Jesus said. What can we make of it?

Doctrine and dedication

First of all, there is a doctrinal lesson here. From these calls for commitment, we must ask the question: 'Who is this Jesus?' Who is it that can call others to put devotion to him above personal welfare and family and all other duties, when necessary?

Jesus is who he says he is – God become man. He is the one to whom we owe our very existence. The deity of Christ is not something tucked away in a few texts, it is right there on the surface of Scripture. Jesus calls for such devotion to him because he is our Maker, our Judge, our Saviour, and our God. Therefore he rightly says: 'Come follow me, come what may. My demands are absolute.'

Secondly, notice the context. Why such commitment? Well, it is involved with the spreading of the kingdom of God (verses 60, 62). As we saw earlier, he is about to send out seventy-two disciples on a mission of the kingdom, taking the gospel, taking his healing to the people. Why must there be such commitment? It is because the things of this world are passing. For all their goodness, they are passing away. Every comfort that we know here is a fading comfort. But there is an eternal kingdom that stands forever. The eternal kingdom must take precedence over that which is only temporary. Why must there be such commitment? It is because people are bound for the terrible, eternal judgment of hell and nothing is more important than that they be saved.

How we can thank God for the remedy, permanence and peace of his kingdom. Not long ago we had a tragedy in our daughter congregation. A dear faithful Christian man had a tragic accident at work in which he lost his left arm. It was a dreadful shock both to him and his wife and the church. But the great comfort of the gospel is that this has not blighted his life forever, because he will be forever with the Lord in a new heaven and a new earth and made whole with a new, glorified body. Life may be tragically difficult here, but life is not only here, this is just the beginning. There is an eternal kingdom which takes precedence over everything in this world. Christ is preparing that place for us and we take it seriously. 'Be committed to my kingdom, to the church which is the vehicle of my kingdom in this world, to the local church which is the vehicle of the kingdom in your particular area,' Jesus would say.

Where do we live?

Perhaps this is where we need to face very practical matters concerning the impact of consumerism and its influence on the decline of the church in many geographical locations of our land. Many inner city and urban areas have gone through a period where they have almost been abandoned by the church. For example, in former days, in places like South London, the great congregation of Spurgeon's church not only gathered on Sundays but had a vast influence on the locality throughout the week, both in gospel witness and works of mercy. Many of the members lived and worked in the area and were part and parcel of the community.

But with the rise of the consumer society and especially the motor car, there has been a departure of people from the cities into the suburbs. This departure has included Christians too. Sadly, in this as in many other avenues of life, the Christians have been little different from their secular neighbours. Churches have both dwindled in numbers attending, and where they have continued to be supported, it has often been through people who drive in from the suburbs and then drive off again after the services. The desire to live in 'a better area' has frequently been the catalyst which has moved Christians away. The idea of 'driving to church' does not only affect inner city congregations. It has become the norm in most churches.

This has left us with a situation in which not only are the churches weak, but also Christian witness and worship is dislocated from the geographical areas of home and work. Thus Christians' lives become fragmented. Where we live, where we work and where we worship are very separate geographically and can therefore be easily treated as separate compartments of our lives. With this compartmentalization it is excessively simple to treat our Christianity as a privatized faith, which does not have to relate firmly to our everyday lives. It is seen as what we happen to choose to do on Sundays. As this situation has evolved, then the foundations have been laid for our relationship to Christ and his kingdom to be viewed as just another consumer item.

Not only has the consumer mindset vitiated our personal faith, but it has also weakened the relevance of the churches to the society around them. We have chosen to pursue living in a nice house. We have chosen to live in a place where you can get a better home for the price you pay. As people have opted for the 'drive in' church, so the churches are no longer as plugged in to their local communities. Living far away from where the church meets, it becomes more problematic for the congregation to be involved in social concern and good deeds which commend Christ and the gospel to the community. Instead of Christians living and worshipping in the local area and their faith being lived out in a context which naturally relates faith and life, there is fragmentation. The people who live in the area of the place of worship only see a lot of cars drive in on Sunday and then drive off. The people who live where the Christians reside only see the cars drive off on Sunday and sometime later drive back. Neither group relates Christians' lives to the love of God manifested through the care of his church. As I say, so much of this dislocation has come about through Christians pursuing what are basically consumer values in housing and comfort. Where is the commitment to Christ who had nowhere to lay his head? Where are the values of the Lord Jesus who was prepared to 'rough it', leaving heaven's glories and coming as a lowly carpenter and wandering preacher for the love of us and the good of God's kingdom? Christians need to face these matters. Growing a church for God takes commitment.

The fear of commitment

We all now think about the fear of commitment. Of course, there is a natural and a right hesitancy before committing ourselves. It is foolish to be reckless. We ought to be thoughtful and know what we are letting ourselves in for, before we sign up to anything in life. There is therefore a right counting of the cost before all proper commitment, and Jesus himself underlines that.

In Luke 14:27 he says: 'And anyone who does not carry his cross and follow me cannot be my disciple.' So it does cost something to be a real Christian. Then he says we must count the cost: 'Suppose one of you wants to build a tower. Will he not first sit down and estimate the cost to see if he has enough money to complete it? For if he lays the foundation and is not able to finish it, everyone who sees it will ridicule him, saying, "This fellow began to build and was not able to finish." ' Jesus in effect is saying, 'I don't want it to be like that with you. If you are on the brink of becoming a Christian, sit down and think carefully about what is involved.' A proper calculation needs to be made. A person needs to ask himself about how serious the issues are. He is to reflect in the light of eternity. There does need to be a forsaking of the pleasures of sin. There will be opposition of various kinds for being a disciple of Jesus. There is a cost. But remember that there is a heaven to be won and a hell to be shunned. When you do that and look at the cost, you will see that no cost is too much. But Christ wants us to know what we are taking on. There should be a proper thoughtfulness about becoming a Christian. Christ does not despise a right hesitancy. He looks for judicial thought and then in the light of eternity a robust commitment. Having made that commitment he wants us to be true to it for the rest of our lives.

Commitment phobia

But it seems to me that in these days of the consumer society, especially among younger folk, there is emerging what I might call commitment phobia. This is something over and above that legitimate hesitancy. There is a phobia of actually nailing our colours to the mast and saying: 'This is where I am going to stand, this is what I am going to do with my life.' There is almost a pathological condition of frantic dread concerning once-for-all choices.

Some Christian counsellors are beginning to recognise this. Listen to Dr. M. Blaine-Smith, the author of *The Yes Anxiety*, about being worried about saying yes to commitments:

> Beyond the normal hesitancy that we all experience, some people have an ingrained fear of commitment. They dread being drawn into any situation where they feel locked in. Their fear of losing freedom is so extreme that they may even sabotage their own effort to reach important goals.[1]

Interesting, isn't it? People want something but they are almost frightened of being fenced in by their success, so they sabotage it.

He writes of these people who having launched out in one direction:

> Soon second thoughts strike with a vengeance. They are consumed with regret over what they are leaving behind and fear over the new obligations ahead. At this point, they often stun others by suddenly pulling out of pledges they have made.[2]

---

1. M. Blaine-Smith, *The Yes Anxiety,* Highland Books, 1996. 2. Ibid

There may be someone verging on that kind of phobia reading this book. It is something that is emerging out of the unstable consumer society. Very often, those who have had difficult family backgrounds and are churned up within themselves feel this nervousness about decisions. They have very few anchors or stable relationships in their lives from which they can assess prospects with a calm attitude. There are so many choices around them and they don't know what to do. They are frightened of being committed.

Yet, as we said at the beginning of the chapter, the most valuable aims in life, the things that matter in life, can only come through commitment. Achieving deep relationships with others or glory for God in his service take dedication. Those real ambitions that mean something about living a life that matters only come through commitment.

There is both a secular form and a religious form of commitment phobia.

The secular form

Why are people so fearful of losing freedom? The answer surely is that all their pleasures are rooted in the here and now, and they have the view that this is the only life they have, and so if they get it wrong, or miss their opportunity, their whole life is ruined. This is the root of panic. Of course, as we live in society, that whole way of thinking can rub off unconsciously on us as Christians. When we are asked the doctrinal question, 'Do you believe in heaven?' we answer 'Yes.' But at another level we can easily fall into thinking and behaving like non-Christians who see no hope beyond this life. So the primary consideration becomes: 'Am I enjoying things? If not, let's change this or go somewhere else, or whatever.' Doubts assail us. 'Perhaps the non-Christian view is right. Perhaps there is no heaven,' we think. We must hedge our bets. And if we are not enjoying things now or if we are not enjoying instant success, we may be wasting our lives. Panic sets in.

But in the New Testament, the primary focus for our pleasure is not *now*. We must take ourselves in hand. We must go back to basic Christianity. Perfect happiness is not now, it is then. Yes, we do know many pleasures of God here, but we also know many tears, many troubles. We know that in heaven all our tears will be wiped away, but within this world we will have trouble, just as Jesus said. The real joy is to come. It is in the fulfilled kingdom of God. I know people ridicule this as pie in the sky when you die. They can ridicule it, but Jesus is risen from the dead and he promised these things. We must take his promises seriously. He does not lie.

That is the attitude with which many New Testament Christians lived. Listen to Paul counting the cost: 'I consider that our present sufferings are not worth comparing with the glory that will be revealed in us' (Rom. 8:18). New obligations might include suffering, might include some of my freedoms being taken away, but to suffer for Christ is glory. Paul again says: 'We do not lose heart. Though outwardly we are wasting away... for our light and momentary troubles are achieving for us an eternal glory that far outweighs them all' (2 Cor. 4:16-17). The first answer to commitment phobia is to fix our eyes on Christ, on heaven, on the kingdom of God.

The religious form

But then there is what I might call the religious form of commitment phobia. The religious form goes something like this: 'God has a perfect plan for our lives (and he does), but that means that my choices must be perfect or I will miss God's will for my life.' What a thought, 'I must make perfect choices.' Thus the panic sets in. So, paralysed with fear over making a mistake, Christians don't do anything, they don't commit themselves to anything. They feel it is better to make no decision than to make a wrong one.

But this way of thinking is unbiblical. Go back to Luke 9. Perhaps that kind of fear was what was behind that central dialogue in verses 59 and 60: 'Let me go and bury my father.' Think about it. If his father was already dead, the man would probably have already been occupied with the funeral and he would not have been there with Jesus. So it may well be that what he was actually saying was: 'Well, look, Lord, let me just wait until my father dies and I sort things out, and then, when the time is right, I will come and follow you.' But the death of his father might be years away. He wanted the call of Christ to come at what he thought was the convenient time or the perfect moment. But the idea that God has a perfect plan for your life should not lead you to think like that. It should not lead you to think that everything must come together in what appears to be the perfect way in your eyes. It should not lead you into fear of decision-making.

In fact, it should lead you in the opposite direction: 'God is so great that as my heart is right with him, he will make sure that I go in the right direction.' It should make us realise that his providence rules over all things, and so even when God's call seems to come at an inconvenient or messy time, he will still work it out for us. Often in Scripture, situations which from a human perspective look less than ideal are actually particularly blessed by God. Think of the circumstances surrounding the birth of the Lord Jesus. At the time Mary is about to give birth, she and Joseph must travel on a journey because of the Roman tax. When they arrive in Bethlehem, all the hotels are full. She ends up in a stable to give birth. It looks like a mess, but in fact it is all in the perfect plan of God.

His sovereign providence should help me realise that he is providing excellent opportunities through situations which may, on the surface, appear less than perfect from my standpoint at the particular time. To wait indefinitely for what we think are more ideal circumstances can just be a lack of faith. As I humbly seek to trust and walk with God he will guide me, so I need not be afraid of making decisions. If somehow I did take a wrong turn, God is so great that he is able to make even that work together for good. Faith in God frees us from this fear of commitment.

One of the most important verses in Scripture for every Christian is Proverbs 3:5,6: 'Trust in the LORD with all your heart and lean not on your own understanding; in all your ways acknowledge him, and he will make your paths straight.' It warns us against foolish, prayerless leaning on our own wisdom. But it encourages us to realize that we should not be afraid of making decisions. As we look to God he will direct our footsteps through life.

The rewards of commitment

The rewards of commitment are great. Commitment to Christ brings eternal life. He was committed to us, he set his face like a flint, resolutely, to go up to Jerusalem to die for the sins of everyone who believes in him. Our sins are taken away, we have eternal life. When his commitment to us as sinners is met by our commitment to him as Saviour, a kind of spiritual 'chemical reaction' takes place. Our sins in the sight of God are dissolved. An unbreakable bond between ourselves and Jesus Christ is forged, so that his victory over death and hell is shared with us. The joyous life of the Holy Spirit enters our hearts. We have eternal life. This is the primary consequence of commitment to Christ. It brings salvation.

I will underline that in another way. It is a great spiritual principle that we imitate the things we worship. We become like the things that we give our lives to. For example, Psalm 115 is a psalm which speaks of the deadness of the idols which the nations worship. The psalmist writes in verse 8: 'Those who make them will be like them, and so will all who trust in them.' By contrast the apostle John declares the wonderful way that the same principle works as we worship Christ. He writes in 1 John 3:2-3: 'Dear friends, now we are children of God, and what we will be has not yet been made known. But we know that when he appears, we shall be like him, for we shall see him as he is. Everyone who has this hope in him purifies himself, just as he is pure.' You either give yourself to idols and you become like a dead idol, or you give yourself to Christ and one day you will be perfectly like him in heaven. But we become more and more like him daily.

Further, as we are committed to Christ and so become like him, we find reward in being enabled to enjoy God himself more. This follows from our entering into a closer relationship, likeness and communion with Christ. C. S. Lewis, in his inimitable way, has great wisdom to impart to us on this matter:

We must not be troubled by unbelievers when they say that this promise of reward makes the Christian life a mercenary affair. There are different kinds of reward. There is the reward which has no natural connection with the things you do to earn it, and is quite foreign to the desires that ought to accompany those things. Money is not the natural reward of love; that is why we call a man mercenary if he marries a woman for the sake of her money. But marriage is the proper reward for a real lover, and he is not mercenary for desiring it. A general who fights well in order to get a peerage is mercenary; a general who fights well for victory is not, victory being the proper reward of battle as marriage is the proper reward of love. The proper rewards are not simply tacked on to the activity, but are the activity itself in consummation. There is also a third case which is more complicated. An enjoyment of Greek poetry is certainly a proper, and not a mercenary reward, for learning Greek; but only those who have reached the stage of enjoying Greek poetry can tell from their own experience that this is so. The schoolboy beginning Greek grammar cannot look forward to his adult enjoyment of Sophocles as a lover looks forward to marriage or a general to victory.... But it is just in so far as he approaches the reward that he becomes able to desire it for its own sake; indeed, the power of so desiring it is itself a preliminary reward.

The Christian, in relation to heaven, is in much the same position as the schoolboy. Those who have attained the everlasting vision of God doubtless know very well that it is no mere bribe, but the very consummation of their earthly discipleship; but we who have not yet attained it cannot know this in the same way, and cannot even begin to know it at all except by continuing to obey and finding

135

the first reward of our obedience in our increasing power to desire the ultimate reward. Just in proportion as our desire grows, our fear lest it be a mercenary desire will die away and finally be recognised as an absurdity.[3]

A theologian of many years ago, Henry Scougal, put it this way:

He who loveth mean and sordid things doth thereby become base and vile; but a noble and well-placed affection doth advance and improve the spirit unto a conformity with the perfections which it loves.[4]

Summing it up in another way, he puts it like this: 'The worth or excellency of a soul is measured by the object of its love.'[5]

What are you devoted to? For so many people in our consumer society, it is material things. There is no weight about them, there is no gravitas about their personality, they are just superficial people, I weep for them. They are the chaff that the wind will blow away in the Judgment. But commitment to Christ brings the weight of his glory into our lives and changes us to enjoy him and to be like him.

What are the rewards of commitment? Listen to the words of Paul at the end of his life: 'I have fought the good fight, I have finished the race, I have kept the faith [commitment]. Now there is in store for me the crown of righteousness, which the Lord, the righteous judge, will award to me on that day, and not only to me, but also to all

3. C. S. Lewis, Quoted in *The Business of Heaven*, Collins, 1984.
4. Henry Scougal, *The Life of God in the Soul of Man*, Christian Focus, 1996, p. 68. 5. Ibid, p. 68.

who have longed for his appearing.' There is the reward of commitment.

May each one of us be committed to Christ practically, in the workings of his church, and in the looking after of God's kingdom and in the spreading of the gospel, and in seeking to serve one another in Christ. May each one of us know that same reward that Paul looked forward to.

CHAPTER 8

CONSUMERISM AND
THE SLOW APOCALYPSE

At the end of the twentieth century there is a profound feeling in the West that somehow our civilization is coming to an end. This may be simply to do with vestigial superstitious ideas regarding the end of one millennium on the calendar and the beginning of another. It may be to do with the unsettling emotions which are stirred by the cultural change which we have already noted is going on in our society. As we saw in chapter 2, the old rationalistic modernism is on the wane and we are seeing the rise of a very subjective outlook which is labelled post-modernism. In his milestone book and TV series of a few decades ago, *Civilization*, Kenneth Clark said, 'If one asks why the civilization of Greece and Rome collapsed, the real answer is that it was exhausted.' There may be that same sense of exhaustion about the people of the last days of our century.

For whatever reason, there is a perception that our Western culture is jaded and has perhaps run its course and in some sense we are facing 'the end'. Some commentators speak of the loss of hope and vitality in the contemporary world. Others talk of society being morally, aesthetically and spiritually bankrupt. Even the great days of TV seem to be over and our viewing teeters continuously on the brink of banality or crudity.

It is interesting that this seemingly failing society is at the same time the consumer society. What are we to make of the fact that with wealth, production and choice at a pinnacle, somehow our society is decaying? What are the connections between these two great distinctives of our times?

The two cities

This is no doubt a subject which could properly deserve years of research and close thought. However, as Christians, such a connection should not surprise us at all. We know that this is God's world and the extent to which a society is founded on things other than God and his laws, to that extent it will be an unstable society whose ultimate demise is inevitable. It is not the city of man but the city of God alone which remains. His is the eternal kingdom (Dan. 2:44; Mark 1:15).

Considering contemporary society, there are surely ways in which we can see connections between cultural decline and the assumptions of consumerism. We might say that consumerism has within it the seeds of its own destruction.

Seeking to live as Christians today, we need to take that warning seriously. If, as we have seen in previous chapters, consumerism can so easily undermine our walk with God and the community life of commitment to the church, then anything which can make us stop and take stock, and encourage us to thoughtfully extricate ourselves from the web of values of godless consumerism, will be of use to our souls and to our witness for Christ.

Let me, therefore, try to briefly suggest a few ways in which the decline and many woes of our contemporary world may be seen as a direct result of the attitudes of consumerism.

1. Consumerism and the earth's resources

We begin by reiterating the obvious ecological point which was made earlier in the book. At the level of the world's materials, the way in which consumer society is gobbling up our planet's resources makes such a society unsustainable in the long term. The Green Movement throughout the world is doing a noble work in highlighting these facts and throwing down the gauntlet to the crass materialism which dominates the aspirations of mankind. It is saying that unless people control their greed, their exhaust fumes and their continual desire for ever increased and more wonderful possessions, we will turn our world into a desert. We are wreaking havoc by our consumerism and the world inherited by our descendants will not be worth having. The Green Movement is right.

Sadly, in our post-modern world of individualism the warning may not be taken seriously enough. Perhaps the ultimate subjectivist would simply reply, 'It's my life that matters to me. I've no children. Why should I forego pleasure on behalf of other people's descendants?'

2. Consumerism and a drop in birth rate

Following on from the last remark we should note that this desire for individual pleasure fostered by a consumer society does lead many people to turn away from the idea of having children and growing a family. Some would say that the individualized, consumer society treads a path therefore which, taken to its conclusion, leads to self-destruction. People are living with happiness now as their primary goal in life. Writing in the early 1990s, the sociologist A. H. Halsey said, 'Few women and fewer men would rationally choose to have children in a world of exclusively short-term egotistical calculation. The costs and foregone satisfactions are too high. Hence rich countries with the modern ethos have declining or incipiently declining populations. (For a stable population there must be a total fertility rate of 2.1 children per woman; Britain has 1.8, West Germany 1.6; Italy and Spain 1.4 or even 1.2). The individualized as distinct from socialized country eventually and literally destroys itself.'[1]

3. Consumerism and the destruction of moral standards

Consumerism is, obviously, profoundly materialistic. There is a strong argument which says that the idea that the physical universe is the only reality (philosophical materialism) inevitably leads to a society that slowly falls apart.

The argument goes something like this: in the early phases of a society in history the force behind moral imperatives comes largely from a belief in God or other supernatural beings. People keep the laws as they believe they are accountable to some being who is mysterious, powerful and beyond their reach. But the dynamic which promotes economic prosperity and higher standards of living arises largely from the conviction that the material world is of primary importance. This same dynamic, however, develops so as to attack belief in the supernatural and

1. A. H. Halsey, foreword to *Families Without Fatherhood*, by Norman Dennis and George Erdos, The Institute for Economic Affairs, 1995.

thereby undermines the authority of moral standards which have enabled the people in the society to work together and to function. This eventually leads to the destruction of the very security and prosperity on which the society was built.

One of the latest proponents of this argument is Anne Glyn-Jones, former Devon Research Fellow at the University of Exeter. In 1996 she published a book entitled *Holding Up a Mirror: How Civilizations Decline*, in which she showed how this thesis has worked itself out already in the different civilizations of Greece, Rome and Medieval Christendom, and is now working itself out in our own Western culture.

A society which is fundamentally materialistic, Glyn-Jones calls a 'sensate' culture. In an interview she gave to a magazine she said, 'I was surprised as I looked at different cultures that having a superior technology does not save a sensate culture from collapse. Greek technology was superior to Roman and Roman technology was superior to that of the barbarians. But they all fell. And we can see a hint of that today in the way our Western, technically superior, cultures have been expelled from Somaliland, Afghanistan, Vietnam and so on. Despite considerably more advanced Western technology, our sensate cultures could not cope, obsessed with individualism as they are, with an enemy prepared to die for a greater good.'[2] Ultimately, a consumer society has nothing worth dying for and is therefore without enough moral fibre to defend itself.

---

2. *The Therapist*, Vol 4, Number 1, 1996, p. 28.

4. *Consumerism and the silent majority*

The vulnerability of the consumer society to decline is also caused by its concern for personal peace and security. The old saying tells us that all that is required for evil to triumph is that good men should keep quiet. Consumerism is the drug which causes ordinary people to fall into moral sleep and remain silent on all kinds of public matters. As long as their little world of peace and relative prosperity is not disturbed they are happy to remain silent. It is against this background of consumer complacency that all kinds of moral relaxation can arise within a country.

The flip side of this is that the consumer society tends to be one which rewards disruptive elements within society. If people make a great fuss and cause much inconvenience or fear within a consumer society, there will be great pressure not to resist unless their demands directly threaten the material well-being of consumers. Rather than pursue a course of difficult confrontation with the disruptive element, the momentum of opinion will generally be along the lines of giving in to demands, buying off the vociferous protesters, and so society can return to the serious business of enjoying itself. Questions tend no longer to be settled using ideas of what is right and what is wrong, but simply in terms of pragmatism, with the goal of maintaining prosperity and peace.

Highly motivated groups within society recognize this vulnerability and are so encouraged to pursue ever more extreme forms of disruption until they get their way. The consumer society is one prepared to sacrifice its ethics on the altar of the material 'feel-good' factor. How long can such a society remain stable?

5. *Consumerism, taxes and government impotence*

Here we look a little at the experience of Britain in the last two decades, but there is a lesson which would be applicable to any country whose people become eaten up by the consumer bug.

Money buys the things you want. The consumer society is a society in which people are concerned to earn as much money as possible. Governments for a consumer society are voted into power on the promises of providing jobs and keeping taxes as low as possible. It is taken as read that the idea of the possibility of increased taxes was what lost the Labour Party the 1992 election in the UK, while Tony Blair swept to power with Labour in 1997 having promised that there would be no increases in taxes.

Alongside this desire to keep taxes as low as possible, we have seen a general increase in the wealth of average wage earners. But in his 1997 book, *Dark Heart: The Shocking Truth About Hidden Britain*, the journalist Nick Davies has set out the way this superficial good news hides a terrible discrepancy. As wages and standards of living have generally increased, the able and gifted, brain-washed by the individualistic 'look after number one' philosophy of consumerism, have left the poorest in society way behind. Let me quote some of the statistics the book exposes:

> The rich have done best. By 1993/4, the wealthiest 5.5 million people in Britain (the richest 10%) were each enjoying a bonus of £650 income for every £1000 they had been receiving in 1979. In other words, as a result of changes in salaries and taxes and benefits, they were 65% better off. This has nothing to do with inflation. These figures have been adjusted to take account of changes in prices. The very rich have simply become much richer.

It is true too, of the mass of other people. By 1993/4, the population of Britain as a whole saw an increase in income of 40% since 1979.... It was only the poorest quarter – 13.7 million – who were left behind.

The Treasury's own figures show that by 1993/4, the 5.5 million people in Britain who had least money (the poorest 10%) were something like £11 a week worse off than they had been in 1979. This took account of all their spending, including housing, and, again, this had nothing to do with inflation.... They were 14% poorer. For every £1000 which had come their way in 1979, they now had only £860.[3]

What Nick Davies' book explores is the shocking lifestyle of abuse and crime that many of the poorest people in our country are caught up in. Here is the heart of desperate drug culture, of teenage prostitution, and the violence of bored young men who see themselves as worthless.

In human terms, how are such problems to be tackled? Whether we believe the answer is in terms of increased education, increased policing, increased social security or increased opportunities for people to get into work, the obvious point is that whichever route a government decides to take, it will need money to invest in such schemes. However, at the same time, the majority in the consumer society is extremely reluctant to allow the government to raise taxes to pay for these things. Any party which toys with the idea of increased taxation has very little chance of getting into power.

This situation then leaves the consumer society in an extremely precarious position. Here is a deprived, depressed and potentially very violent underclass, but at the same

---

3. Nick Davies, *Dark Heart: The Shocking Truth About Hidden Britain*, Chatto & Windus, London, 1997.

time politicians have their hands tied behind their backs, through lack of finance, to thoroughly address the problem. This may seem a distant and theoretical argument to the wealthy evangelical living in some leafy suburbia in middle-England. But to folk living on the many infamous housing estates throughout the country it is an ever present nightmare.

Here again we see the consumer society as one which seems to carry within it the seeds of its own destruction.

Babylon is fallen

Consumerism is extremely comfortable. It charms us and consoles us at every turn. It has the effect of putting us to sleep and telling us 'not to worry, you're all right, aren't you?' But for all its claims, the consumer society is peddling a false sense of security. The reality is that though it seems so secure and immovable, not being based on God and his ways, it is bound to fall.

This may seem impossible to us in our generation, as we see what seems to be the almighty power of multi-national companies, news organizations, financial markets and international banks. Yet surely the idea that Rome, 'the eternal city', could fall would have seemed equally impossible to the people of the early Christian centuries. But fall it did to the barbarian hordes. It had become complacent and self-indulgent. On the night of 24th August 410, the unthinkable happened. Alaric stormed the walls of the city in a surprise attack and pillaged it for three days. For the first time in 800 years Rome had fallen to a foreign army.

The Christian is to see that outside the city of God is

man's city of Babylon. But Babylon is doomed to destruction (Revelation 18) and God's call is to come out of it:

> 'Come out of her, my people,
>> so that you will not share in her sins,
>> so that you will not receive any of her plagues;
> for her sins are piled up to heaven,
>> and God has remembered her crimes' (Rev. 18:4,5).

This call to come out from the consumer society is not a call to withdraw ourselves physically into some secluded monastery in which we have no contact with the society around us. Neither are we to withdraw into some super-spiritual evangelical ghetto, forgetful of the world. We must engage with the world. We are called to be witnesses for Christ within our culture. But it is a call to come out from the spirit and values of consumer Babylon. For our generation it is a call to cultivate a heart and lifestyle of Christian contentment.

CHAPTER 9

THE SHOCKING IMPACT OF A CONTENTED CHRISTIAN

Please read Philippians 4:10-13

<blockquote>
[10]I rejoice greatly in the Lord that at last you have renewed your concern for me. Indeed, you have been concerned, but you had no opportunity to show it. [11]I am not saying this because I am in need, for I have learned to be content whatever the circumstances. [12]I know what it is to be in need, and I know what it is to have plenty. I have learned the secret of being content in any and every situation, whether well fed or hungry, whether living in plenty or in want. [13]I can do everything through him who gives me strength.
</blockquote>

Have you ever had that experience of writing a letter and after you have written a sentence it dawns on you that it doesn't sound quite right. You think, 'I had better explain that, they might take it in the wrong way!' I think Paul must have felt something like that when he wrote verse 10: 'I rejoice greatly in the Lord that at last you have renewed your concern for me.' He quickly goes on to add: 'Indeed, you have been concerned, but you had no opportunity to show it.'

Philippians is a joyful missionary's 'thank you' letter

to a supportive congregation. Paul is in Rome in prison for his faith, and he is expressing his gratitude to the Christians at Philippi for the gifts and help they have sent him in this time of need. But those words 'at last' in verse 10 could so easily have been taken the wrong way. They could have understood him to be having a moan and implying, 'It's a pity you did not send it before!'

So Paul writes to clarify what he is getting at and the nub of it is that he was more concerned for them than he was about himself and his own needs. He was waiting longingly, not for their gifts as such, but for news of their Christian faith. Their gifts would be an evidence that they were going on with Christ and indeed a token that they were growing as Christians. Generosity is always a good sign of Christians progressing towards maturity and pleasing God. 'Not that I am looking for a gift,' writes Paul in verse 17, 'but I am looking for what may be credited to your account.'

Thus, careful to dispel any thought of personal chagrin or disappointment over the time delay of their aid to him, he inserts an explanatory parenthesis in verses 11-13. And this parenthesis becomes a very impressive statement of Paul's contentment as a Christian. 'I am not saying this because I am in need, for I have learned to be content whatever the circumstances. I know what it is to be in need, and I know what it is to have plenty. I have learned the secret of being content in any and every situation, whether well fed or hungry, whether living in plenty or in want. I can do everything through him who gives me strength.'

It was so important for the Philippians to understand Paul and it is equally important for us to understand and embrace the vital lesson of Christian contentment. As we come to the close of these observations on living in a consumer culture, this matter of learning contentment in Christ is the most crucial lesson of all, and we will use these verses to address the subject under five headings.

1. The Importance of Christian Contentment

A great deal could be said, but I will highlight just one thing. As a pastor of a church I have fairly often had to face the questions, 'How are Christians meant to be different in today's society? How can we give a distinctive testimony in the way we live today?'

As I have thought about it, I have realized that although mature Christian character is a fixed goal, in the sense that we all must aim to become like Christ who is the same yesterday, today and forever, yet as the times and scenery of history change, it will be different aspects of Christian character which will particularly stand out against the background of the world at different times. Over against the changing shades of culture, although the whole Christian character is being pursued, different aspects of that character will become prominent, come to the fore, and become the cutting edge of a clear testimony at different periods.

Let me give you an example of what I mean. If we went back to the days of Nazi Germany with all its violence and racism and intolerance, how would true Christians stand out? Their love and their gentle acceptance of people would have been a dramatic contrast to the society surrounding them. That would have been very much a cutting edge of witness. But if we come up to the present day in the West, the whole atmosphere is different. Ours are days of multi-culturalism. Everyone in society, at least superficially, is in favour of love and tolerance. The back-cloth has changed. We live in different times. This particular aspect of Christian character of love does not stand out so much.

So where has the cutting edge of witness and the distinctiveness of Christian lifestyle in the West shifted to now?

Along with the need for a loving purity of life in a decadent culture, I believe with all my heart that it is this matter of contentment which is the required cutting edge.

We live in the age of consumerism. There is a continual concern for higher and higher standards of living, even to the detriment of the ecology of the planet. We are exposed to a vast and sophisticated advertising industry which continually and deliberately seeks to massage discontent. It tells the individual constantly, 'You need more.' In an age in which the whole direction of people's lives is domin-ated by climbing the career ladder, acquisition of material goods and never being satisfied, for a Christian to be able to honestly say, 'I am fine as I am, I don't need anything,' is a tremendous and glorious shock to the non-Christian's system. It is the cutting edge. To be known as an able colleague and yet to have no greater ambition than to be content in God, is so astonishing, it makes people sit up.

It is as shocking as finding an old, imprisoned and neglected apostle of a despised religion, and finding that he is totally at peace and aglow with a heavenly joy despite all his circumstances. No wonder the news of Christianity spread throughout the palace guard in Rome (Phil. 1:13). This man was like no other prisoner they had ever known!

Usually they were morose and full of understandable complaints. But this man's cell was a place of joy. To make that kind of impact on our neighbours and colleagues in our consumer culture, a heart filled with Christian contentment is the key.

Of course, Christian contentment is vitally important for other reasons too. It is a blessing personally. 'But godliness with contentment is great gain. For we brought nothing into the world, and we can take nothing out.... For the love of money is a root of all kinds of evil. Some people, eager for money, have wandered from the faith and pierced themselves with many griefs' (1 Tim. 6:6-10).

But here, let us simply note that it is contentment which will make an impact for Christ. By contrast, to be concerned to be rich will not only lead you into spiritual trouble, but will convince the world that you are no different from them.

2. The Nature of Christian Contentment

Paul writes: 'I have learned to be content whatever the circumstances. I know what it is to be in need, and I know what it is to have plenty. I have learned the secret of being content in any and every situation, whether well fed or hungry, whether living in plenty or in want' (Phil. 4:11,12).

What is this contentment which Paul is speaking of? How can it be described?

This contentment is an inward and personal thing. That is plain from Paul's statements that his contentment is something which is independent of his outward circumstances. Our contemporary society focuses much time and attention on material goods and outward surroundings, but contentment is a matter of the heart. It

153

has to do with a Christian's soul rather than his or her surroundings.

The word Paul uses for 'content' in verse 11 has the meaning of 'needing no assistance' or 'able to support oneself.' A new-born baby cannot stand up on its own. It has to have someone to support it if it is going to stand with feet on the ground. But as it grows, it is strengthened. Perhaps as a little toddler it learns to stand holding itself up against a chair or another piece of furniture. The strength is still not there to stand alone. But eventually with time and growth, the day comes when the youngster can stand up without anyone or anything else supporting. That can be taken as a picture of a Christian soul coming to maturity. Christ gives an inner strength (verse 13), and the Christian learns, and eventually, whatever the circumstances, the Christian can stand contented with no visible means of support from circumstances.

From the prison context in which the letter was written and from the surrounding verses such as verses 4-7, we can see that this contentment, this inner strength, is redolent of the joy, peace and trust in God and his sovereign disposal of our circumstances. 'Rejoice in the Lord always' (verse 4). 'Do not be anxious about anything, but in everything, by prayer and petition, with thanksgiving, present your requests to God. And the peace of God, which transcends all understanding, will guard your hearts and your minds in Christ Jesus' (verses 6,7).

Christian contentment is the inner peace and joy from God and trust in his over-ruling goodness, which enables the Christian to be at ease with himself and his situation, any time, anywhere.

This is to be contrasted with worldly contentment. There is a contentment which the world knows and seeks. But it is to do with outward circumstances and possessions, and being in control of the situation oneself. It is to do with outward things and therefore is very vulnerable and fragile. Christian contentment by contrast is not dependent on finances, career prospects, or the luxury of our surroundings. It is inward.

The Puritan Jeremiah Burroughs likens the world's contentment to an old man keeping warm. He does it through lots of coats, scarves and jumpers, layers and layers, put over himself. But the contentment of a Christian is like the warmth of young healthy teenagers; they do not need all this outer clothing, because they have life and warmth generated inside their bodies. They are strong and warm within.

It is God's desire that each of his children should know this inner warmth of contentment through their knowledge of him.

3. The source of Christian contentment

Where does this strength, this inner peace and sufficiency come from? Paul writes: 'I can do everything through him who gives me strength' (verse 13). We can draw out a couple of points here.

First, it is worth underlining that this contentment is to do with a strength which is put within us by the Lord. It is true that when we become weak, sick or tired, it is then that we are most prone to discontentment and perhaps taking out our discontent on other people. When Paul is weary, it is then that his prison surroundings seem most irksome. When we have had a tiring day at the office, then we are most prone to be ratty with others. When we have gone to bed too late, we often feel low and a bit blue the next day. In such situations God does give strength through Christ. It is a spiritual strength which uplifts the inner person through a knowledge of him and his love.

Second, this strength for contentment comes not from ourselves, but from Christ. 'I can do everything through him who gives me strength.' This is what distinguishes Christian contentment from mere Stoicism or self-discipline. There may be some good in those things, but they are fuelled by a person's own strength of will, their own strength of character. There is no other energy source and that is why, though there may be some good in them, they are bound to fail.

But the Christian knows a source of strength from beyond himself. The Lord Jesus, risen and ascended into heaven, who has been given all authority in heaven and on earth, gives his people strength. This is what enables a Christian to be at peace whatever the circumstances or the battles.

The strength which Christ gives takes different forms.

It may be *mental* strength mediated to us through a better grasp of biblical doctrine. God uses his Word to enlighten us and to see our circumstances in a new light. It could be a new view of the sovereignty of God which enables us to realize afresh that our times and situations are in his hands and he works all things together for the good of his people. This helps us not to be depressed, but to have a hope.

It may be *emotional* strength. Sometimes the inner witness of the Holy Spirit, testifying to our spirit that we are the children of God, no matter what others think of us, brings a new joy to our hearts. This, in turn, gives us new determination to continue along a difficult path for Christ.

Sometimes it may even be *physical* strength which the Lord gives. We read in Scripture of various occasions when the Spirit of God endued people like Elijah or Samson with physical energy. And God is able to do the same today as and when he wills.

Christ himself, through his Spirit, is the source of strength. He is the one who mediates inner peace and fortitude to the soul. We need to be close to him in our Christian lives.

4. The acquisition of Christian contentment

How does this strength from Christ, which brings inner contentment, come to us? It is worth noticing that Paul twice says that contentment is something he learned (verses 11, 12).

First, the tenses of the verbs used here indicate that this was not something that slowly dawned on Paul over a long period of time. Rather it was a secret he was initiated into, something he recognised in an instant. It broke upon him at his conversion when he first met Jesus Christ and saw him in his divine majesty and grace and surrendered his life to him. Christ and Christ alone is the only one who is able to give us contentment.

Second, we need to go on and realize that the secret which Paul learned in an instant when he met Christ has to be applied practically to our lives. Paul learned how to foster and nurture a relationship of living trust in and obedience to Christ, and so continually to experience the inner strength which Christ can give. The writer to the Hebrews instructs his readers who are finding the Christian race tough to 'fix your eyes on Jesus' and to 'consider him... so that you will not grow weary and lose heart' (Heb. 12:2,3). There must be a continual communion *with* and contemplation *of* Christ. Bluntly, contentment comes through the spiritual exercises of prayer and meditation on God's Word and all it says of Jesus. Those who wait on the Lord are those who renew their strength (Isa. 40:31). In a consumer society which tells us that only what we can experience through the five physical senses is of any use, we need to realize that the most valuable thing we can do is to spend time alone with the Lord Jesus.

Paul learned how to trust the Lord Jesus in the bad times. He had learned before he got to prison, that very often what appears to be a setback, God can use as a way of promoting the gospel (Phil. 1:12,13). The word translated 'need' in 4:12, where Paul speaks of learning to be content in times of need, can be translated as 'abased'. It is the word used of Jesus 'humbling' himself in chapter 2:8. In the difficult times, Paul fixed his eyes on Jesus, and knew the fellowship of Christ, knowing that Christ had walked similar paths before him.

Paul learned as well how to trust Christ and be obedient to him in the good times. There were times when Paul had plenty (verse 12). When those times came, he was able to enjoy them knowing that his Lord and Master is the maker and provider of all things. With this in mind he was kept from pride or rebellion during those times of plenty. He was enjoying the plenty, but still very aware that he was absolutely dependent on Christ. Hence he continued to walk closely with the Lord and to draw his inner strength from him.

5. The usefulness of Christian contentment

These verses in Philippians 4 show us Paul content in every kind of circumstance. This meant that he was in a position to be useful to God in every situation. The strength he enjoyed through Christ did not only bring him contentment, but enabled him to 'do everything through him who gives me strength' (verse 13).

Because he was strengthened inwardly and content in Christ, he was extremely useful to Christ. Because he was not worried about his social status or his living conditions, Paul was a man prepared to go anywhere, meet anyone, and do anything for Christ's sake. The cause of Christ is in short supply of such people in the consumer age. Perhaps what is required by many Christians is a rededication of their lives to the Lord Jesus Christ.

I am reminded of the life of the great missionary, C.T. Studd. He dated his conversion from his middle-teenage years, when a visitor called Weatherby visited the family home. C.T. Studd went on to university, and as a great cricketer for England became a household name throughout the land for his sporting achievements. However, though a Christian and well-known, his life made very little impact for Christ. It was not until he was twenty-four-years old that this really changed.

Beginning to take his walk with God more seriously, he was led to see the need of not keeping anything back from God. In his room in London, he began to seek God. He wrote: 'I had known about Jesus Christ's dying for me, but I had never understood that if he died for me, then I didn't belong to myself.' That is quite a lesson, which is particularly pertinent to Christians in a consumer society which encourages us to own as much as possible, with never a thought about who owns us. C.T. Studd continues: 'Redemption means "buying back", so if I belonged to him, either I had to be a thief and keep what wasn't mine, or else I had to give up everything to God. When I came to see that Jesus Christ had died for me, it didn't seem hard to give up all for him. It seemed just common, ordinary honesty.'[1]

Convinced that 'I had kept back myself from him and had not wholly yielded', C.T. Studd prayed sincerely to God that he would take his life and accept it as wholly dedicated to Christ. From that time in September 1884, C.T. Studd had what one biographer describes as 'peace, security, overflowing contentment and a willingness to go wherever he was sent'. This change in Studd shocked his sporting friends. Contented and fully surrendered to Christ, he had a new edge. This contented man, like the apostle Paul, became a very useful person for Christ.

What now?
Here we see what God is calling us to, he tells us to 'come out' of the consumer culture which tends to dominate the nations and even the church in the West.

We are to be distinguished from the world around us in a variety of ways. We are to be holy people. And a crucial part of that holiness in the present generation is to have our hearts filled with strength from Christ, which brings a

1. John Pollock, *A Fistful of Heroes*, Christian Focus, 1998.

peaceful contentment with our circumstances.

It is through Christ that we can find a contentment to make the consumer society sit up and take notice. God challenges us to be markedly different. He challenges this generation of Christians to change. He is challenging us to abandon the false security of the acquisitive lifestyle. Christ's church needs to be set free from the fetters of consumerism and so be able to glorify God before an astonished world in the coming years.

CHAPTER 10

CHRISTIANITY, CONSUMERISM
AND CONCLUSIONS

As we have surveyed the subject of consumerism and the questions it poses for Christian discipleship, we have had to look at many different aspects of contemporary life for the individual and society. In some ways consumerism is like the Hydra of ancient mythology; it is a beast with many heads. Yet we have to conquer the challenges which consumerism is putting before us as Christians at the turn of the second Christian millennium.

Given the varied nature of consumerism and its challenges, this final chapter seeks to draw together an overview and to give a short summary of the areas we have covered.

Primarily Christians have to recognize that the culture of the Western world has changed markedly in the last thirty to forty years and continues to change at an alarming rate. We need to be aware that we have become the so-called consumer society.

The secular gospel

Consumerism is the current good news or gospel which is offered by secularism to the world. We called consumerism the secular gospel because it pretends to hold out good news of great joy to people – well, at least to the prosperous anyway. It issues a promise of happiness through acquiring

163

material goods and services, which focuses particularly on the pleasure people get from exercising personal choice.

It is the aspect of personal choice which differentiates consumerism from old-fashioned materialism. People have always enjoyed acquiring things, there has always been a tendency to live for the material world instead of God. If we have enough 'things' we feel that we are secure and even self-sufficient. But even the rich fool in Jesus' parable in Luke 12 did not have the vast multitude of options with which our society confronts us as to what we can spend our money on. To take just one example, I saw a statistic recently that the Revlon cosmetics company makes 177 different shades of lipstick. What an amazing range to choose from! There may be seven primary colours, but there are 177 ways in which people can colour their lips.

We enjoy this acquisition and choosing. It has been said that we have to consume to live, but now we live to consume. Shopping, choosing, spending and acquiring is the stuff of life for many people now. As self-centred people we like owning things. To own things is perhaps the nearest we can get to feeling godlike. To own is to have power. But there is more to it than that. As society has grown numerically, and as it has become increasingly urbanised with people living in vast towns and cities, life has become increasingly anonymous. The village community, where everyone knew and accepted one another, is gone. People do not get the recognition they used to have. In such an anonymous society, personal choice in clothes or music or diet etc., is a way of making a statement about oneself. My clothes or my music speak to others about who I am. This is another reason why people get a buzz from the personal choice of consumerism. It is an avenue of self-expression.

Given the comparative wealth of the Western world, this emphasis on personal choice and making a statement about "who I am", fits hand in glove with the contemporary post-modern mindset of subjectivism where the only truth is what is 'true for you'.

As Christians we can see that materialism and self-centredness are forms of idolatry. However, we must be careful not to over-react. To think that the material world is inherently evil is a form of Gnostic heresy which we find condemned in Scripture (1 Tim. 4:3-5). The material world is not evil in and of itself. God made the material creation and became incarnate, taking to himself a material body in Jesus Christ (1 Tim. 3:16). Further the final state of our redemption is not some 'see through' ethereal state. According to Scripture it includes the resurrection of the body and the renewal of the material universe (Rom. 8:22-25).

But though we are not to over-react and condemn the material creation over against materialism and consumerism, as Christians we believe that we can only use the material world properly as it leads us to be thankful to God and to order our lives in loving worship of him (1 Tim. 4:4). This does not come naturally to sinners.

TV - the prophet of consumerism
Marshall McLuhan was the great guru of sociology in the 1960s. His most famous saying was 'the medium is the message'. In other words the very method by which a message is communicated to us is a message in itself. We can understand this simply by thinking about speech as a

165

method of communication. Our words are the message, but our tone of voice is the medium through which the message is sent. We all know that we can completely change the meaning of a set of spoken words just by altering the tone of voice in which they are expressed. The words 'O yes' can be shouted with joy by a sports crowd as they watch their team score. The same words can be spoken in an inquisitive tone by a suspicious headmaster to a naughty little pupil and mean something totally different. No longer are the words an expression of delight, now they are questioning or even condemnatory in their meaning.

In just this way the TV, which is now so much a part of everyday life in the developed world, has messages in and of itself just because of the medium which it is. Above and beyond a programme's content there are ideas communicated by the TV itself. We can sum up the most important of these messages like this.

- TV is Visual – its message is 'what you see is what is true', implying material reality is all there is.

- TV is Instant – it captures the attention. Now is the only time that matters. If we are into a programme our capacity for inner reflection is temporarily shut down.

- TV is Distant – though we see things on the television, the things we see cannot directly hurt us. People may starve or be blown up, but not us. This blunts our moral sensitivity.

■ TV is Entertaining – it delights our eyes. Pleasing the viewer is the most important thing. Subtly the idea that life is about pleasure is communicated to us.

■ TV is Optional – it provides a vast variety of programmes and channels to watch, and puts a control in our hands and says in effect, 'You choose.'

Putting all this together we can see that in a strange way TV in and of itself brings the basic messages of consumerism. It is materialistic in that it tells us that reality consists of what is seen. It tells us that enjoying yourself now, not moral concerns, is the most important thing in life. It panders to the idea that personal choice is a top priority for us all. Every day therefore people are preached at by consumerism. Even apart from the adverts, the TV preaches, in the most entertaining and fascinating way, the basic tenets of consumerism to people. Rich and poor alike are nurtured on this gospel, which each day comes right into their homes.

How consumerism affects individuals

As this message of consumerism goes out into all the world people are affected by it. It shapes the way people think and make their decisions. Consumer ideals set the priorities in life for most people. Let us just list a few ways in which individuals are affected.

Our world-view. People are led to set their priorities in terms of this life only. Matters of eternity and of the spiritual side of personal existence are of less importance to people as they are overwhelmed by the materialistic propaganda of consumerism. This attitude can rub off to a certain extent even on Christians. Serving the Lord is important, but no longer as important as it was to previous generations who had a far clearer view of eternity.

Our values. Many of the open values of consumer culture cut directly across Christian virtues. We know that the fruit of the Spirit includes patience (Gal. 5:22-23). But the ethos of the credit card society says, 'Why wait ? Get what you want now!' Again self-denial is part of Christian discipleship. Jesus tells us that we must deny ourselves, take up the cross and follow him. But consumer society tells us not to deny ourselves anything; rather, before anything else, life is about enjoying yourself. The Christian sees that joy has its place; but joy in God and giving joy to God by our trust and obedience, and not the fleeting pleasures of the material world, is to be our guiding rule.

Our goals. The theologian David Wells has shown recently that whereas in previous centuries there was a concern to develop human character, our society is taken up with developing personality.[1] What is the difference? Character is an inner disposition to love what is good, with 'good' being defined in absolute terms by the nature and will of God. The people of the past, especially Christians, would strive to grow in love and holiness as their goal in life to the glory of God. In contemporary society, secularism reigns, God is dead, and the idea of moral absolutes has all but gone. Now, therefore, people are far more attracted to the idea of feeling good about themselves and becoming 'interesting' or 'stylish' or 'fun' personalities. It does not

---

1. David Wells, *Losing Our Virtue*, IVP, 1998.

matter so much whether you are morally straight, so long as you are exciting to be with. A good image will win friends and influence people and help you on your way through life far more than being concerned to be holy. Of course, consumer products and ideas stand close by to aid us in every endeavour to be interesting and attractive people. The shift has been made from the inner life to the outward image.

Our identity. This is very closely connected to the last point and operates at a very deep level. In the past our identity, as defined by such things as gender, religion and social class, determined many of our choices. For example, women would wear some kinds of jewellery, men would wear something different. Religious people used Sundays in one way, whereas non-religious people used it differently. Working class people went to certain places on holiday and middle class people went to different resorts. But now we live in a society in which identity is seen as a much more fluid thing. In a sense we can choose our identity. All we have to do is to buy the appropriate status symbols. But this means that personal identity is devalued. It is just an image. Hence people today have difficulty knowing who they really are. Also since identity is such a fluid thing, any links between who we claim to be and expected moral behaviour are loosened. They are not to be taken too seriously for, who knows, we may change our minds about who we want to be next week. This vitiates serious Christian discipleship.

How consumerism affects the church

Not only does the consumer culture shape the way we think and act as individuals, but also because the church is made up of individuals, if those individuals are influenced, it will also begin to influence the church. In this way, the tenets of consumerism can begin to rule God's flock, rather than the Word of God. Here are some of the areas where this can happen.

Our message. The biblical gospel is the message which the church is to take to the world. That gospel is fundamentally good news concerning the forgiveness of sins before a holy God, through the Lord Jesus Christ and his cross. Christ Jesus came into the world to save sinners (1 Tim. 1:15). This message assumes a God-centred moral framework to the world and defines 'good' in moral terms. The culture of consumerism has grown up in an atheistic/ secular society which has abandoned absolute moral categories. It has redefined 'good' as a therapeutic entity. It is that which makes people feel better and brings healing. There is therefore immense pressure on preachers to change the church's message, recasting it in man-centred terms. The new gospel would see salvation primarily in terms of self-fulfilment rather than salvation from righteous wrath. It is a message which sees mankind basically as victims, rather than agents of sin who need to repent. Ultimately this is a mindset in which God himself is viewed as a consumer item, to be brought out of the cupboard when we are feeling hurt or in need, and put away again when we no longer need him.

Our community. Consumerism is very individualistic. It is all about us acquiring things. To own things is to have power as an individual. Consumerism also concerns our personal choice. It centres on 'me'. By contrast God is calling us away from isolated individualism into his family, the church. He wants to see participation and caring involvement with other people. He wants to see us exercising our gifts for the common good (1 Cor. 12:5). Here again, the basic attitude of consumerism is at loggerheads with the revealed will of God. The new commandment which Jesus gave to his disciples is to love one another. As he has loved us, with all the sacrifice of Calvary, so we are to love one another (John 13:34).

Our commitment. Consumerism majors on personal choice and therefore in a consumer world the idea of 'keeping your options open' becomes a virtue. 'Whatever you do, do not shut down your opportunities to choose – this is the stuff of life,' the secular gospel tells us. However, when keeping our options open becomes a continual state of mind, commitment and perseverance inevitably die. Keeping your options open is the same as continually sitting on the fence. When this attitude rubs off on Christians, churches are used as a kind of spiritual supermarket, where we shop to get our personal needs met, but that is all we are interested in. We go to get, not to give. Often, when the going gets tough in a church (and it always does at some point, for we have an enemy, the devil), people withdraw and go to 'shop' elsewhere. This is not the view of the church we find in the New Testament. Obviously, we need to choose a church, but having done so, we need to stick with it and get lovingly involved in the family of God.

Our worship. The ethos of our consumer society is set by TV and the post-modern concern with image rather than content. Together these are powerful influences which push even Christians towards being more concerned with how things look, or 'come over', rather than how they actually are. In particular, it is easy for Christians to view church as a piece of stage-managed theatre rather than a true time of engagement with God. We could find ourselves becoming twenty-first century Pharisees, taken up with outward appearance rather than inner spiritual reality (Matt. 23:25-28; Mark 7:6).

Why consumerism is a deception

There is only one true gospel. It is the good news about God's Son, the Lord Jesus Christ, who died that we might be forgiven and have eternal life. Though there is nothing wrong with material things in themselves, the approach to them purveyed by consumerism is an idolatrous lie. The nations are being deceived.

Deceiving individuals. Consumerism minimizes almost to zero the relevance of God, moral values, holy desires and the quest for spiritual character. It tells us that life is solely about personal enjoyment, with conscience or the Bible way down the list of things which ought to shape our lives. But we are moral beings, made in the image of God whether we acknowledge it or not. Therefore we cannot be at ease with ourselves by ignoring this area of our lives. We cannot find peace by suppressing the conscience or ignoring God. The statistics which show a great rise in cases of depression and the use of tranquillizers in our generation are surely not unrelated to this.

People are deceived by consumerism at an even deeper level according to the Bible. Material things, though good, cannot satisfy our souls. There is a spiritual void in the hearts of fallen men and women which no amount of acquisition and ownership can fill. The richest man in the Bible, King Solomon, warns us as he writes, 'The eye never has enough of seeing, or the ear its fill of hearing' (Eccl. 1:8). Jesus said, 'Man does not live on bread alone' (Matt. 4:4). In so saying, he condemned the secular gospel of consumerism as a deception.

But consumerism misleads the world even beyond this. Though they can never satisfy the soul in this life, the vast array of goods and services which are offered to people take their attention. Consumerism causes people to focus on the here and now, and to forget God and to forget eternity. Jesus lamented for rich people who were never at a loss to find things to distract them in this life. They would weep. Having neglected God, and having had no time for his Son and salvation, they would be shut out of the kingdom of heaven (Luke 6:20-26). Jesus' words still ring true, 'What does it profit a man, if he gains the whole world, but loses his soul?' (Mark 8:36).

Deceiving society. The consumerist lifestyle and the industries which sustain it gobble up the earth's resources at an alarming rate. We are living in a fool's paradise if we think that the world can go on living the high-tech, throw-away, pleasure-centred lifestyle forever. Blatant consumerism is not a sustainable way of life for the world.

Consumer society is a complacent society. 'Let people do what they want so long as it doesn't threaten our enjoyment.' That is the attitude of the mass of consumers.

But that in and of itself brings an instability into society. The flip side of that complacency is that the consumer society rewards disruptive elements who threaten the peace and prosperity of the majority. In that way, while revelling in its luxurious stupor, consumerism actually encourages certain elements in society to be disruptive and even violent.

Similarly it is the experience of the last thirty years that in a consumer society there is less and less willingness in people to pay taxes to central government. People have been brainwashed into feeling that the only really worthwhile use of their money is to spend it on themselves. They do not want what they see as the government 'taking our money'. This short-term and self-centred view of personal finances has meant that whereas society in the West is wealthier than it has ever been, the quality of such things as our education, emergency services and public health care is struggling, if not in decline. There are many warnings that these services are coming close to breaking point. But it is these very services which in many ways act as the glue of a society and make citizens feel that it is worthwhile to be regular members of society. If these services are neglected and fail, some people may come to the conclusion that there is little point in cooperating with the state. This leads again to the destabilisation of society. The Bible tells us that Babylon, the metaphor for luxurious man-centred civilization, is a city which is built on insecure foundations and will always fall eventually.

Over against the deceptions of consumer society, the apostle Paul turns us back to God. 'People who want to get rich fall into temptation and a trap and into many foolish and harmful desires that plunge men into ruin and

174

destruction. For the love of money is a root of all kinds of evil' (1 Tim. 6:9-10). Rather the Christian lifestyle should be characterized by better ways which lead to better things. 'Godliness with contentment is great gain' (1 Tim. 6:6). This was God's wisdom for his children in the first Christian century. It is still God's wisdom for us today.

John Benton is the editor of the monthly Christian newspaper *Evangelicals Now*. He is the author of several books, including *Losing Touch With the Living God* and *Straightening Out the Self-centred Church*. John lives in Guildford in southern England where he is pastor of a Baptist church.